Moulton College

NORTHAMPTONSHIRE

Profit through Skill

GOLF COURSES

getmapping® + HarperCollins*Publishers*

GOLF
COURSES

AMAZING VIEWS FROM
www.getmapping.com

First published in 2002 by
HarperCollinsPublishers
77–85 Fulham Palace Road
London W6 8JB

The HarperCollins website address is:
www.fireandwater.com

Photography © 2002 Getmapping plc

Getmapping can produce an individual print of any area shown in this
book, or of any area within the United Kingdom. The image can be
centred wherever you choose, printed at any size from A6 to 7.5 metres
square, and at any scale up to 1:1,000. For further information, please
contact Getmapping on 0845 0551550, or log on to www.getmapping.com

The publisher regrets that it can accept no responsibility for any errors
or omissions within this publication, or for any expense of loss thereby
caused.

A CIP catalogue record for this book is available from the British Library.

ISBN: 0 00 714413 X

Text by Ian Harrison
Design Colin Brown/Martin Brown
Photographic image processing by Getmapping plc
Printed and bound by Editoriale Johnson, Italy

contents

6   LOCATION MAP

7   SOUTHERN ENGLAND

32   EAST ANGLIA & THE MIDLANDS

46   NORTHERN ENGLAND

84   SCOTLAND

110   WALES & NORTHERN IRELAND

128   INDEX

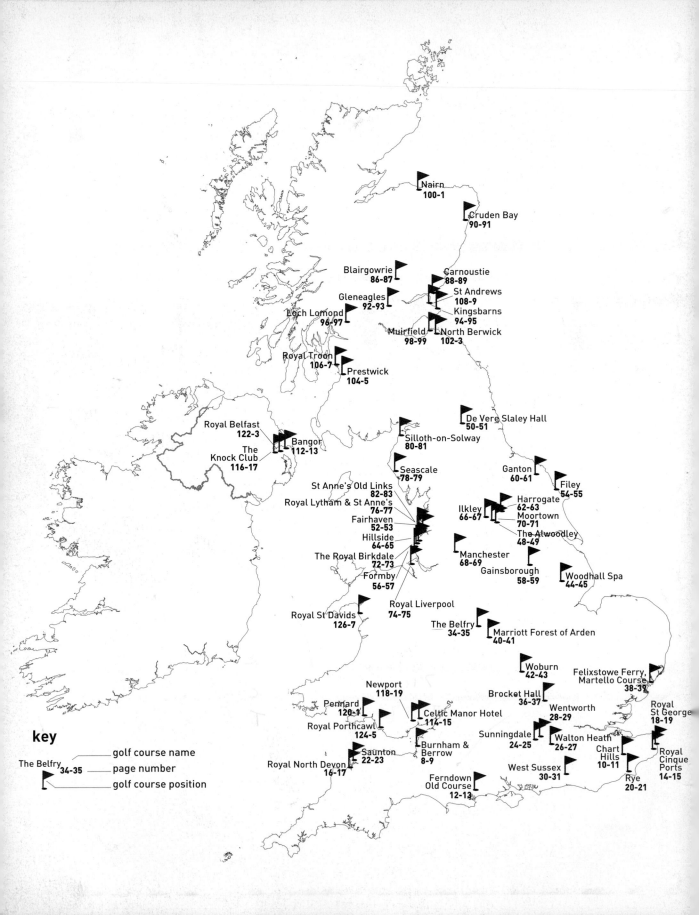

Nairn
100-1

Cruden Bay
90-91

Blairgowrie
86-87

Carnoustie
88-89

Gleneagles
92-93

St Andrews
108-9

Loch Lomond
96-97

Kingsbarns
94-95

Muirfield
98-99

North Berwick
102-3

Royal Troon
106-7

Prestwick
104-5

De Vere Slaley Hall
50-51

Royal Belfast
122-3

Bangor
112-13

Silloth-on-Solway
80-81

The Knock Club
116-17

Seascale
78-79

Ganton
60-61

Filey
54-55

St Anne's Old Links
82-83

Royal Lytham & St Anne's
76-77

Harrogate
62-63

Ilkley
66-67

Moortown
70-71

Fairhaven
52-53

The Atwoodley
48-49

Hillside
64-65

Manchester
68-69

The Royal Birkdale
72-73

Gainsborough
58-59

Woodhall Spa
44-45

Formby
56-57

Royal Liverpool
74-75

Royal St Davids
126-7

The Belfry
34-35

Marriott Forest of Arden
40-41

Woburn
42-43

Felixstowe Ferry,
Martello Course
38-39

Brocket Hall
36-37

Newport
118-19

Wentworth
28-29

Royal
St George
18-19

Pennard
120-1

Celtic Manor Hotel
114-15

Sunningdale
24-25

Walton Heath
26-27

Royal Porthcawl
124-5

Burnham &
Berrow
8-9

Saunton
22-23

Chart
Hills
10-11

Royal
Cinque
Ports
14-15

Royal North Devon
16-17

West Sussex
30-31

Rye
20-21

Ferndown
Old Course
12-13

key

The Belfry 34-35

golf course name

page number

golf course position

SOUTHERN ENGLAND

BURNHAM & BERROW

Burnham-on-Sea, Somerset

1. Club founded: 1890
2. Course architect: Unknown
3. Type of course: Links
4. Length (yards): 6606
   Length (metres): 6041
5. Par: 71
6. SSS: 73
7. Membership: 800

England Photographic Atlas:
Page 76, A2

Tel: (01278) 785760

Burnham & Berrow is unusual in having a church at its centre, and the course has been altered over the years in an effort to avoid church-goers being hit by stray shots. At the same time, the alterations to the layout have given the course a more open feel, with the removal of several blind shots – although the decision to remove these shots has been criticised for "reducing a little the glorious uncertainty of golf". Burnham & Berrow is renowned for its deceptive slopes, small steep greens, and for its orchids.

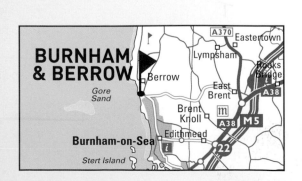

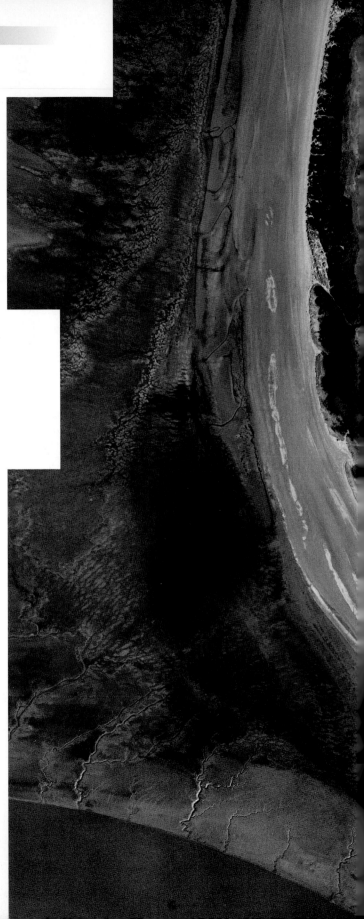

Location:
1 mile north
from the centre
of Burnham-
on-Sea

CHART HILLS

Ashford, Kent

1. Club founded: 1993
2. Course architect: Nick Faldo/Steven Smyers
3. Type of course: Parkland, open country
4. Length (yards): 7135
   Length (metres): 6524
5. Par: 72
6. SSS: 74
7. Membership: 400

England Photographic Atlas : Page 177, C5

Tel: (01580) 292222
www.charthills.co.uk

Just as great footballers don't necessarily make great managers, so great golfers don't necessarily make great course architects – but at Chart Hills Nick Faldo (in consultation with American Steve Smyers) has proved that it is possible to be both. Chart Hills has been favourably compared with some of the greatest courses in the world, aspects of Faldo's course being described by golf writer Nick Edmund as "reminiscent of Royal Melbourne" and "providing a hint of Pine Valley", with "steep revetted pot bunkers similar to Carnoustie and Muirfield". The only complaint from some purists (apart from the high green fees) is that the course is slightly fussy, with a little too much sand and water.

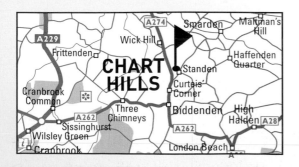

Location:
12 miles west
from the centre
of Ashford

FERNDOWN OLD COURSE

Bournemouth, Dorset

1. Course laid out: 1914 (formally opened 1921)
2. Course architect: Harold Hilton (reclaimed by Sir Henry Webb)
3. Type of course: Heathland
4. Length (yards): 6452
   Length (metres): 5895
5. Par: 71
6. SSS: 71
7. Membership: 700

England Photographic Atlas : Page 66, D5

Tel: (01202) 874602
www.ferndown-golf-club.co.uk

Rated by Peter Alliss as one of his favourite courses, the Ferndown Old Course was first laid out by Harold Hilton (Open Champion 1892 & 97) from 1912–14, when the heathland was drained and sown and the fairways cut through the conifers and pine trees. Almost after immediately it had opened, the course was abandoned for the duration of the Great War, and was reclaimed by Sir Henry Webb from 1920–21, after which a 1920s handbook described the course as "a really fine one, providing, as nearly as an inland course can, the golf to be found on first class seaside links – a really good test of golf for all classes of player."

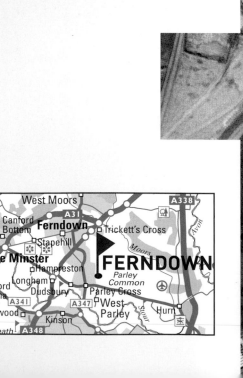

Location:
6 miles north
from the
centre of
Bournemouth

ROYAL CINQUE PORTS (DEAL)
Deal, Kent

1. Club founded: 1892
2. Course architect: Tom Dunn/Guy Campbell
3. Type of course: Links
4. Length (yards): 6482
   Length (metres): 5927
5. Par: 72
6. SSS: 71
7. Membership: 1000+

England Photographic Atlas : Page 205, G3

Tel: (01304) 374007
www.royalcinqueports.com

Royal Cinque Ports Golf Club describes its course at Deal as "undoubtedly one of nature's masterpieces", although nature has not always been kind to the club – having hosted the Open in 1909 and 1929, Royal Cinque Ports was prevented from doing so again in 1949 because the sea flooded the links. The course is laid out along a narrow strip of dune-land alongside the English Channel and, like all early links courses, it runs out along the seashore and returns to its starting point further inland on a parallel run. Golf writer Bernard Darwin commented that "golf at Deal is very good indeed – fine, straight-ahead, long-hitting golf wherein the fives are likely to be many and the fours, few." The club is proud to say that his description remains true.

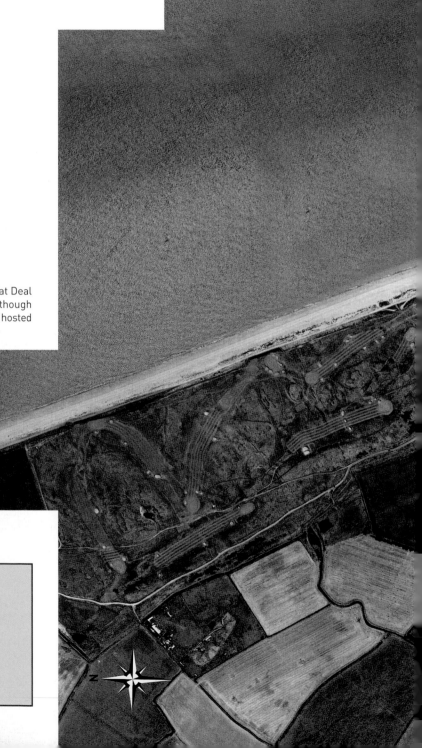

Location:
2 miles north
from the centre
of Deal

ROYAL NORTH DEVON (WESTWARD HO!)
Bideford, Devon

1. Club founded: 1864
2. Course architect: Old Tom Morris ("fine-tuned" by Herbert Fowler, 1908)
3. Type of course: Links
4. Length (yards): 6653
   Length (metres): 6083
5. Par: 71
6. SSS: 72
7. Membership: 1100

England Photographic Atlas : Page 68, B3

Tel: (01273) 473817
www.royalnorthdevongolfclub.co.uk

The oldest links course in England, Westward Ho! is famous for looking simple and flat but being deceptively hard to play. As well as the tight fairways, deep bunkers, natural grassy mounds and patches of sea gorse, an additional hazard is that sheep wander freely on the course, and except on competition days the greens are encircled with orange tape to protect them from ovine attention. The course was originally laid out by Old Tom Morris but his design has been described as "pretty primitive" and was improved upon by Herbert Fowler in 1908.

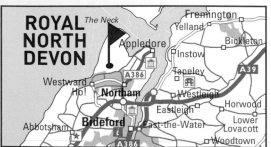

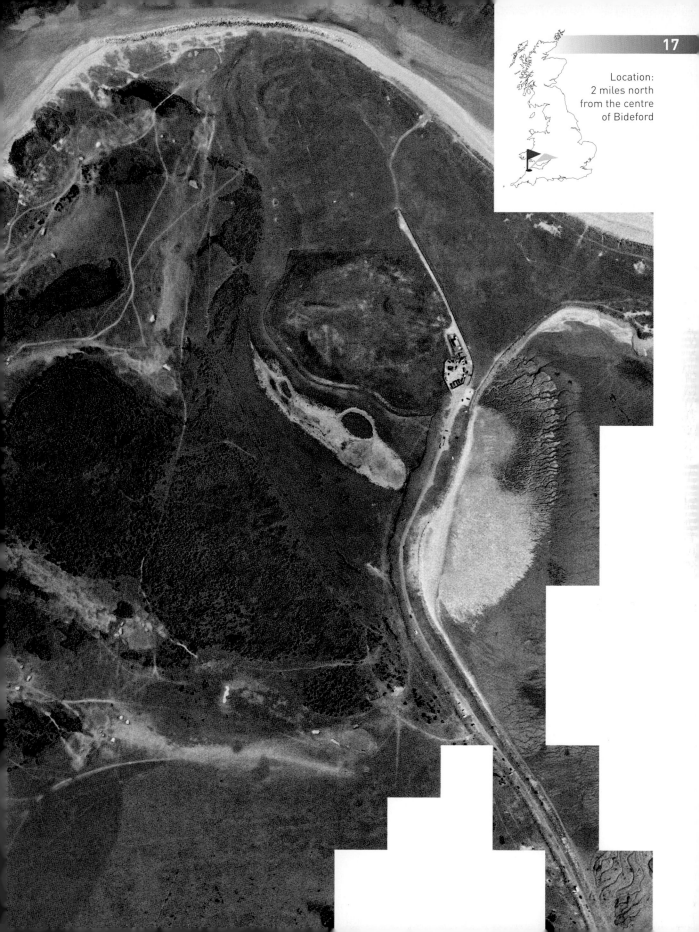

Location:
2 miles north
from the centre
of Bideford

ROYAL ST GEORGE'S
Sandwich, Kent

1. Club founded: 1887
2. Course architect: Dr W Laidlaw Purves
3. Type of course: Links
4. Length (yards): 6610
   Length (metres): 6044
5. Par: 70
6. SSS: 72
7. Membership: 675

England Photographic Atlas :
Page 205, F1

Tel: (01304) 613090
www.royalstgeorges.com

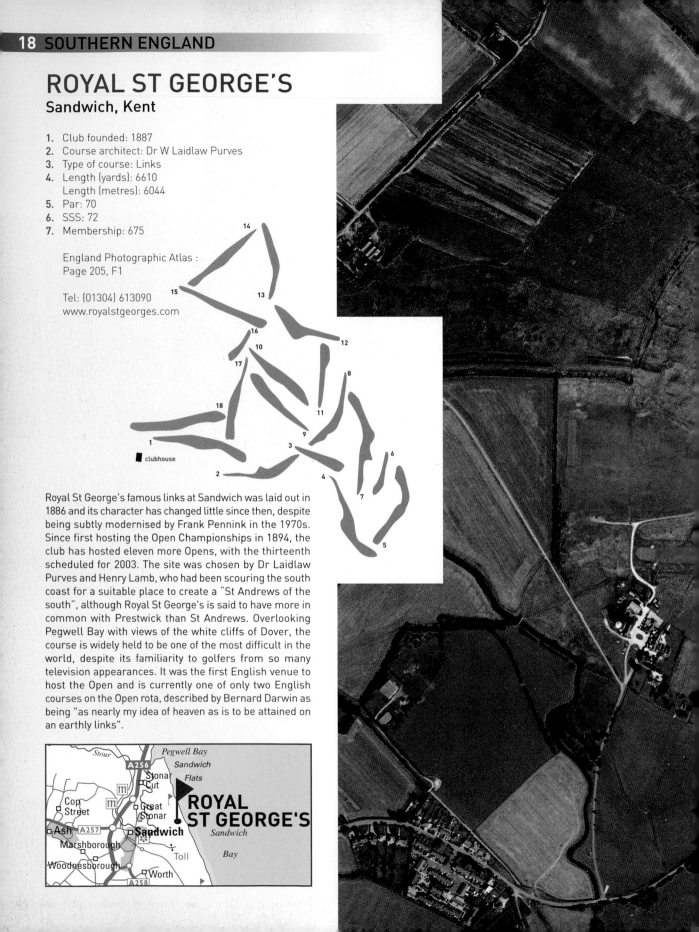

Royal St George's famous links at Sandwich was laid out in 1886 and its character has changed little since then, despite being subtly modernised by Frank Pennink in the 1970s. Since first hosting the Open Championships in 1894, the club has hosted eleven more Opens, with the thirteenth scheduled for 2003. The site was chosen by Dr Laidlaw Purves and Henry Lamb, who had been scouring the south coast for a suitable place to create a "St Andrews of the south", although Royal St George's is said to have more in common with Prestwick than St Andrews. Overlooking Pegwell Bay with views of the white cliffs of Dover, the course is widely held to be one of the most difficult in the world, despite its familiarity to golfers from so many television appearances. It was the first English venue to host the Open and is currently one of only two English courses on the Open rota, described by Bernard Darwin as being "as nearly my idea of heaven as is to be attained on an earthly links".

Location:
1 mile east from
the centre of
Sandwich

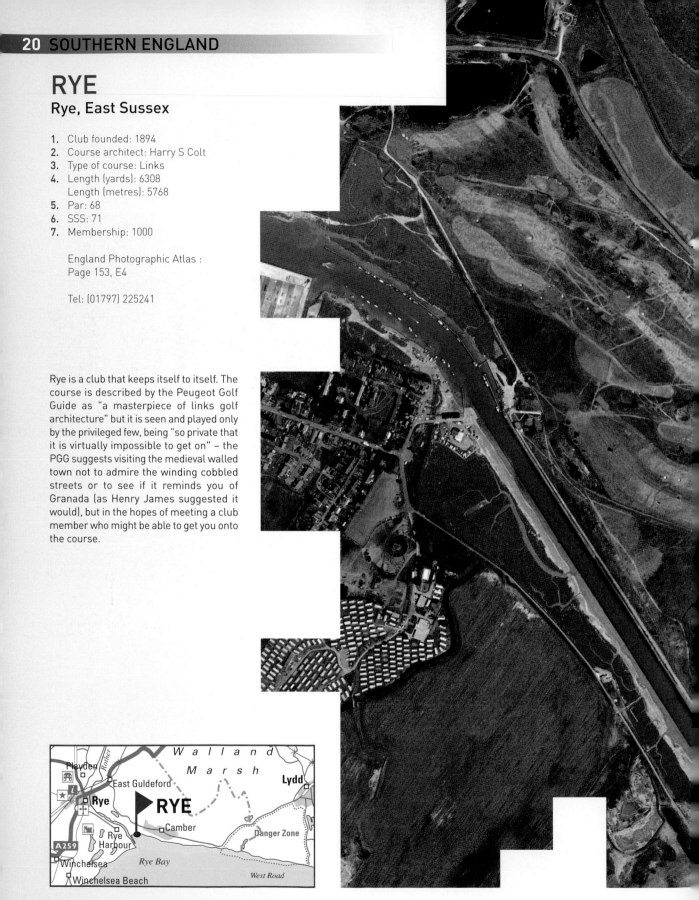

RYE
Rye, East Sussex

1. Club founded: 1894
2. Course architect: Harry S Colt
3. Type of course: Links
4. Length (yards): 6308
   Length (metres): 5768
5. Par: 68
6. SSS: 71
7. Membership: 1000

England Photographic Atlas :
Page 153, E4

Tel: (01797) 225241

Rye is a club that keeps itself to itself. The course is described by the Peugeot Golf Guide as "a masterpiece of links golf architecture" but it is seen and played only by the privileged few, being "so private that it is virtually impossible to get on" – the PGG suggests visiting the medieval walled town not to admire the winding cobbled streets or to see if it reminds you of Granada (as Henry James suggested it would), but in the hopes of meeting a club member who might be able to get you onto the course.

Location:
3 miles east
from the
centre of Rye

SAUNTON
Barnstaple, Devon

1. Club founded: 1897
2. Membership: 1250

EAST COURSE

1. Course laid out: 1897
2. Course architect: Herbert Fowler
3. Type of course: Links
4. Length (yards): 6729
   Length (metres): 6153
5. Par: 73
6. SSS: 73

WEST COURSE

1. Course laid out 1972–75
2. Course architect: JJ Pennink
3. Type of course: Links
4. Length (yards): 6403
   Length (metres): 5855
5. Par: 71
6. SSS: 71

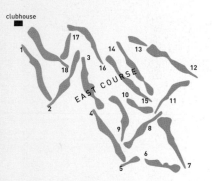

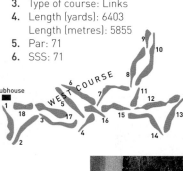

England Photographic Atlas : Page 70, D6

Tel: (01271) 812436
www.sauntongolf.co.uk

Harry Vardon wanted to retire to Saunton, and it is a course that attracts high praise – Colin Callender, Editor of Golf Monthly, rates it as "probably the finest 36 holes of links golf in the British Isles" outside St Andrews, and Henry Longhurst described it as "the finest course never to have hosted the Open Championship". The two courses, East and West (the East being the recognised Championship course), are laid out on Braunton Burrows between Saunton Sands and the Taw and Torridge estuary, with the river, sea and sands providing a beautiful backdrop.

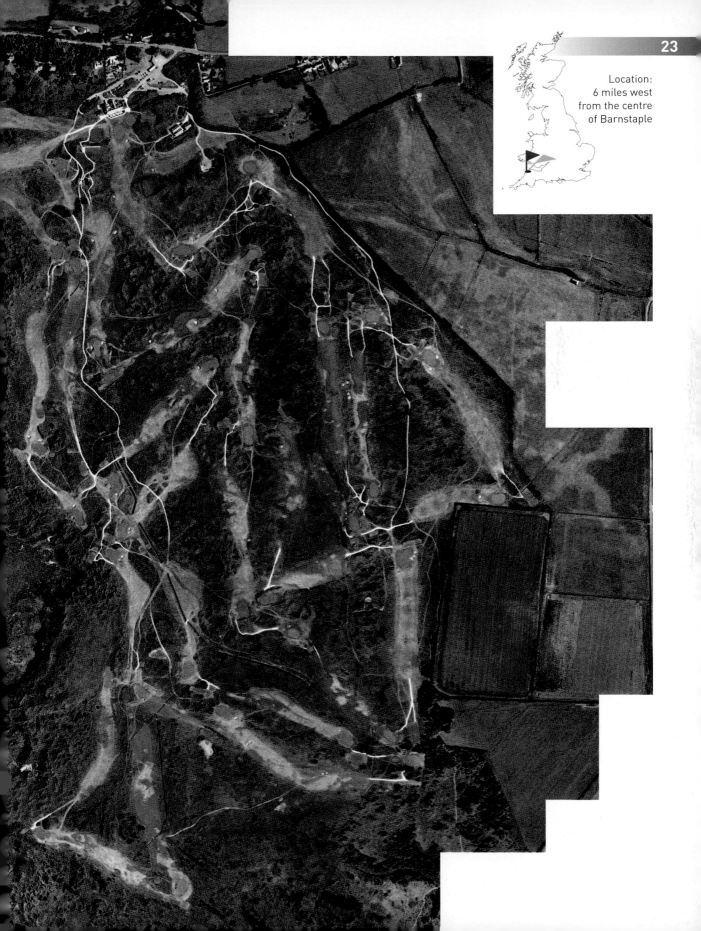

Location:
6 miles west
from the centre
of Barnstaple

SUNNINGDALE

Sunningdale, Berkshire

1. Club founded: 1900
2. Membership: 900

OLD COURSE

1. Old Course completed 1901
2. Course architect: Willie Park Jr
3. Type of course: Heathland
4. Length (yards): 6581
   Length (metres): 6017
5. Par: 72
6. SSS: 72
7. Membership: 900

NEW COURSE

1. Course laid out: 1923
2. Course architect: Harry S Colt
3. Type of course: Heathland
4. Length (yards): 6617
   Length (metres): 6050
5. Par: 71
6. SSS: 73

England Photographic Atlas : Page 190, C2

Tel: (01344) 621681
www.sunningdale-golfclub.co.uk

Described as one of Willie Park Jr's masterpieces, the Old Course at Sunningdale acquired its prefix when the New Course was opened in 1923. The Old Course is laid out on sandy soil with 103 bunkers, and is lined with pine, birch and oak trees culminating in the final green below the famous "Sunningdale Oak Tree"', the emblem of the club. The course includes what is said to be golf's first man-made water hazard on the approach to the 5th, and the 10th was described by Peter Dobereiner as "one of the most magnificent holes in Britain, or indeed the world". The Old Course was the scene of Bobby Jones's legendary round of 66 while qualifying for the 1926 Open Championship, which he went on to win – his feat of 33 shots and 33 putts was described at the time as the perfect round. The New

OLD COURSE

NEW COURSE

Location:
8 miles
southwest from
the centre of
Staines

Course is not so heavily bunkered or tree-lined as the Old but has more heather and tighter fairways. Although it has not seen as many great moments as the Old Course, it was the scene of Gary Player's first victory as a professional, when Sunningdale hosted the Dunlop Masters in 1956. The New Course has exhilarating views across the wild landscape of Chobham Common.

WALTON HEATH
Surrey

1. Club founded: 1903
2. Membership: 900

NEW COURSE
1. Course laid out: 1907–13
2. Course architect: Herbert Fowler
3. Type of course: Heathland
4. Length (yards): 6609
   Length (metres): 6043
5. Par: 72
6. SSS: 72

OLD COURSE
1. Course laid out: 1904
2. Course architect: Herbert Fowler
3. Type of course: Heathland
4. Length (yards): 6801
   Length (metres): 6219
5. Par: 72
6. SSS: 73

England Photographic Atlas :
Page 169, F1

Tel: (01737) 812380
www.whgc.co.uk

Walton Heath Golf Club was founded by Sir Cosmo Bonsor and his son, and both courses were designed by Herbert Fowler, who was related to the Bonsors by marriage. The Old Course was opened in 1904 with an exhibition match between Harry Vardon, James Braid and J.H. Taylor and, nearly a hundred years later, it is still ranked as one of the top 100 courses in the world. In the days when politicians had time to play golf, many MPs played here, including Winston Churchill and Lloyd George, and the club also has its royal connections: The Prince of Wales (later Edward VIII and then Duke of Windsor) was Club Captain in 1935, and the Duke of York (later George VI) was an honorary member. The "New" Course is less than a decade younger than the old and, like the old, was designed by Herbert Fowler, who is quoted as saying "God builds golf links, and the less man meddles the better for all concerned". Walton Heath is not a links course but it has been compared with one. In his Guide to Golf in Great Britain, Peter Dobereiner said, when discussing links and inland golf "There is no reconciling the opposing views, but if ever the twain should meet, it would surely be at Walton Heath". Members claim that the New Course is two shots easier than the old.

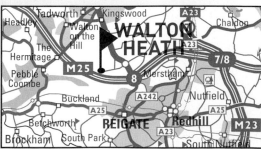

OLD COURSE
NEW COURSE

Location:
2 miles north
from the centre
of Reigate

WENTWORTH
Surrey

1. Club founded: 1924
2. Membership: 3622

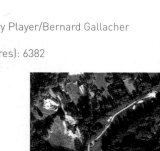

EAST COURSE
1. Course laid out: 1924
2. Course architect: Harry S Colt
3. Type of course: Forest
4. Length (yards): 6176
   Length (metres): 5647
5. Par: 68
6. SSS: 70

WEST COURSE
1. Course laid out: 1926
2. Course architect: Harry S Colt
3. Type of course: Forest
4. Length (yards): 6957
   Length (metres): 6361
5. Par: 73
6. SSS: 74

EDINBURGH COURSE
1. Course laid out: 1990
2. Course architect: John Jacobs/ Gary Player/Bernard Gallacher
3. Type of course: Forest
4. Length (yards): 6979   Length (metres): 6382
5. Par: 72
6. SSS: 73

England Photographic Atlas :
Page 190, D1

Tel: (01344) 842201
www.wentworthclub.com

Covering 200 acres of the Wentworth estate, including the castellated 18th-century country house that serves as the clubhouse, Wentworth was founded by Walter George Tarrant who bought the estate and called in Harry S Colt to design two courses – the East opened in 1924 and the West two years later, with a third course (Edinburgh), joining them in 1990. The West Course is the most famous of the Wentworth courses, familiar to millions through the PGA and World Match-Play Championships which are held here annually. The West Course only came to prominence in the 1950s, before which the East Course was considered to be Wentworth's premier course. The East course has not had the same attention as the West but the drier, sandier soil, the heather, and the less tricky layout all make for what many golfers find a more enjoyable course.

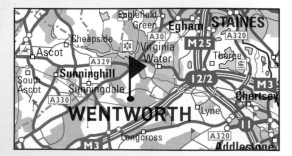

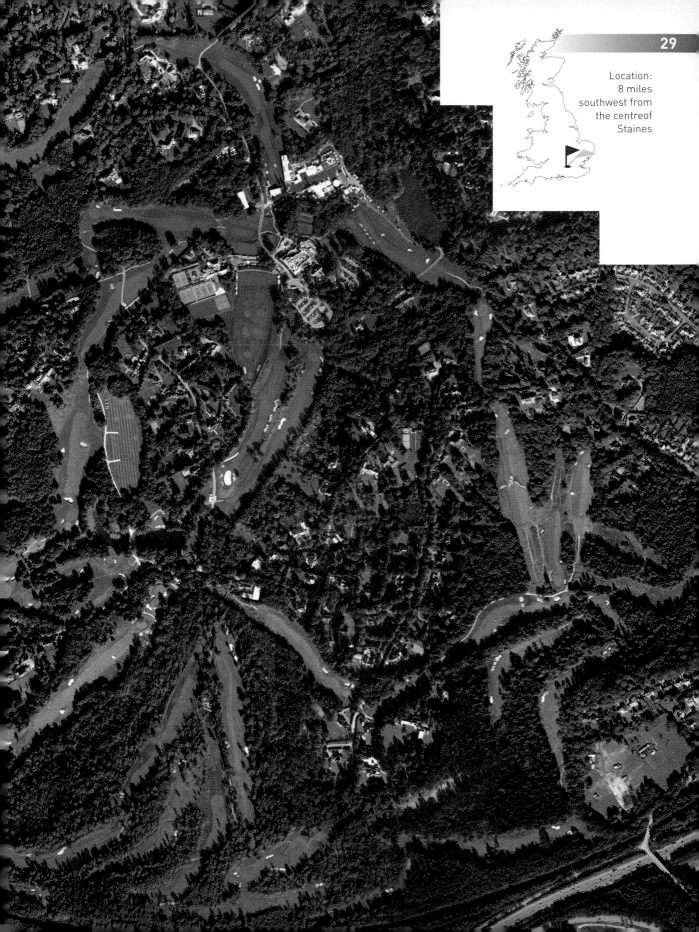

Location:
8 miles
southwest from
the centreof
Staines

WEST SUSSEX (PULBOROUGH)
Pulborough, West Sussex

1. Club founded: 1930 (Officially opened 1931)
2. Course architect: Guy Campbell/Cecil K Hutchinson
3. Type of course: Heathland
4. Length (yards): 6223
   Length (metres): 5690
5. Par: 68
6. SSS: 70
7. Membership: 800

England Photographic Atlas : Page 145, G5

Tel: (01798) 872563
www.westsussexgolf.co.uk

The West Sussex Golf Club, also known simply as "Pulborough", has been described as "an absolute gem of a course" and, although it features in the top 100 courses in the British Isles, is considered to be hugely under-rated with the true quality of the course a well-kept secret. The club describes the course at Pulborough as "an outstanding beautiful heathland course occupying an oasis of sand, heather and pine in the middle of attractive countryside which is predominantly clay and marsh", with the 6th and the 13th rated by Sir Peter Allen, in his book "Play the Best Courses", as the two best inland holes in the British Isles.

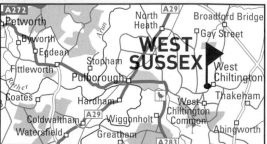

Location:
1.5 miles east
from the centre
of Pulborough

EAST ANGLIA & THE MIDLANDS

THE BELFRY

Warwickshire

1. Club founded: 1977
2. Membership: unknown

BRABAZON COURSE

1. Course laid out: 1977
2. Course architect: Peter Alliss
   (remodelled by Dave Thomas)
3. Type of course: Open country, parkland
4. Length (yards): 7118
   Length (metres): 6508
5. Par: 72
6. SSS: 74

PGA NATIONAL COURSE

1. Course laid out: 1997
2. Course architect: Dave Thomas
3. Type of course: Open country, parkland
4. Length (yards): 6737
   Length (metres): 6160
5. Par: 72
6. SSS: 72

DERBY COURSE

1. Course laid out: 1977
2. Course architect: Peter Allis
   (remodelled by Dave Thomas)
3. Type of course: Open country, parkland
4. Length (yards): 6009
   Length (metres): 5495
5. Par: 70
6. SSS: 69

England Photographic Atlas : Page 437, H4

Tel: (01675) 470033
www.devereonline.co.uk

In 2001, The Belfry became the first venue to host the Ryder Cup four times, and is almost as famous for its top-class facilities as for the courses themselves. During the 1970s the Belfry was created as the new headquarters of the British PGA, and there are now three courses twisted round each other in this convoluted site: the famous Brabazon Course, scene of the Ryder Cup action; the PGA National, which is expected to improve as the saplings grow (as was the case with the Brabazon); and the Derby, which supposedly caters for "every standard of golfer". Architect Dave Thomas's brief for the Brabazon was to create an American style course and in that he succeeded, the course being described by Nick Edmund as "a slice of Florida in England". The Brabazon provokes extreme and diametrically opposed reactions in critics, being denigrated by some for providing insufficient challenge or excitement and praised by others for producing dramatic and exciting golf.

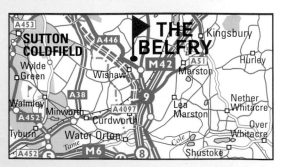

Location:
2 miles north
from junction 9
of M42

BROCKET HALL

Welwyn, Hertfordshire

1. Club founded: 1992
2. Membership: 580

MELBOURNE COURSE
1. Course laid out: 1992
2. Course architect: Peter Alliss/Clive Clark
3. Type of course: Parkland
4. Length (yards): 6616
   Length (metres): 6047
5. Par: 72
6. SSS: 72

PALMERSTON COURSE
1. Course laid out: 1999–2000
2. Course architect: Donald Steel
3. Type of course: Woodland
4. Length (yards): 6925
   Length (metres): 6047
5. Par: 73
6. SSS: 73

England Photographic Atlas : Page 294, B6

Tel: (01707) 390063
www.brocket-hallgolfclub.co.uk

The two championship courses at Brocket Hall are named after 19th-century Prime Ministers who owned this 543-acre estate. Lord Melbourne, whose grandfather bought Brocket Hall in 1746, was made Prime Minister in 1832, and Melbourne's brother-in-law, Lord Palmerston, inherited the estate in 1848. The Melbourne Course features four holes that cross the water of the Broadwater Lake and the River Lea, including the magnificent finishing hole at which the Brocket Hall ferry transports golfers across to the green. In 2000, the Melbourne was complemented by the opening of the Palmerston, a course that cuts through the beautiful woodland of the estate with tight fairways, huge bunkers and USGA specification greens.

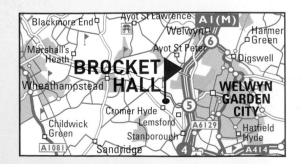

Location:
1 mile west
from the centre
of Welwyn
Garden City

FELIXSTOWE FERRY, MARTELLO COURSE
Felixstowe, Suffolk

1. Club founded: 1880
2. Course architect: Tom Dunn (1880)/John Baird (1920)/
   Henry Cotton & Sir Guy Campbell (1947)
3. Type of course: Links
4. Length (yards): 6308
   Length (metres): 5768
5. Par: 72
6. SSS: 70
7. Membership: 850

England Photographic Atlas : Page 315, E5

Tel: (01394) 286834
www.felixstowegolf.co.uk

Felixstowe Ferry Golf Club was founded as the Felixstowe Golf Club by Lord Elcho MP, and for the first four years of its existence, the guardroom of the Martello Tower served as the clubhouse. John Baird's original course was badly damaged during the Second World War and was reconstructed in 1947 by Henry Cotton and Sir Guy Campbell, becoming known as the Martello Course. The club was re-established the following year after the wartime break, adopting its new title of Felixstowe Ferry. Earl Balfour, who was Captain of the original Felixstowe GC in 1889 and Prime Minister from 1902-05, is quoted as saying "Give me my tools, my golf clubs and leisure, and I would ask for nothing more. My ideal in life is to read a lot, write a little, play plenty of golf, and have nothing to worry about."

Location:
2 miles
northeast from
the centre of
Felixstowe

MARRIOTT FOREST OF ARDEN

West Midlands

1. Club founded: 1970
2. Membership: 650

ARDEN COURSE
1. Course architect: Donald Steel
2. Type of course: Parkland
3. Length (yards): 6718
4. Length (metres): 6142
5. Par: 72
6. SSS: 73

AYLESFORD COURSE
1. Course architect: Donald Steel
2. Type of course: Parkland
3. Length (yards): 6525
4. Length (metres): 5966
5. Par: 72
6. SSS: 71

England Photographic Atlas : Page 456, B4

Tel: (01676) 522335
www.marriotthotels.com/cvtgs

The Marriott Forest of Arden Hotel is the centrepiece of a golfing resort set in the midst of the 10,000-acre Packington Estate less than 10 miles from Coventry, and boasts two 18- hole courses, the Arden and the Aylesbury. In June 2002 the English Open was played on the Arden championship course, which has been described in such lukewarm terms as "pleasant", "technically very interesting" and "tricky".

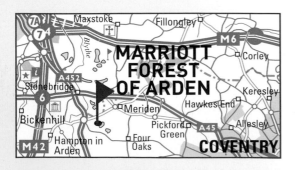

Location:
9 miles west
from the centre
of Coventry

WOBURN
Buckinghamshire

1. Club founded: 1976
2. Membership: unknown

DUKE'S COURSE
1. Course architect: Charles Lawrie
2. Type of course: Forest
3. Length (yards): 6973
4. Length (metres): 6376
5. Par: 72
6. SSS: 74

MARQUESS COURSE
1. Course architect:
   Alliss/Clark/McMurray/Hay
2. Type of course: Forest
3. Length (yards): 7224
4. Length (metres): 6605
5. Par: 72
6. SSS: 74

DUCHESS COURSE
1. Course architect: unknown
2. Type of course: Forest
3. Length (yards): 6651
4. Length (metres): 6082
5. Par: 72
6. SSS: 72

England Photographic Atlas: Page 305, E5

Tel: (01908) 370756
www.woburngolf.com

Of the three courses at the Woburn Golf and Country Club, Duke's is the oldest and the highest-rated, and is the home of the British Masters and a regular host of the Women's British Open. The course is considered slightly flat but the beautiful forest setting of pines and chestnuts, with heather and gorse providing additional hazards, is ample compensation. The Duchess is slightly shorter than the Duke's, but is rated as equally challenging, and both were voted in the top 100 UK courses by Golf World. The youngest of Woburn's three courses is the Marquess, which was opened in 1999 and hosted the British Masters in 2001.

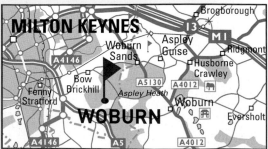

Location:
5 miles
southeast from
the centre of
Milton Keynes

DUKE'S COURSE

DUCHESS COURSE

MARQUESS COURSE

clubhouse

WOODHALL SPA

Lincolnshire

1. Club founded: 1905
2. Membership: 475

HOTCHKIN COURSE
1. Course laid out: 1905
2. Course architect: Col SV Hotchkin
3. Type of course: Heathland
4. Length (yards): 7074
   Length (metres): 6468
5. Par: 73
6. SSS: 75

BRACKEN COURSE
1. Course laid out: 1995
2. Course architect: Donald Steel
3. Type of course: Heathland
4. Length (yards): 6735
   Length (metres): 6158
5. Par: 73
6. SSS: 74

England Photographic Atlas: Page 375, F4

Tel: (01526) 352511
www.woodhallspagc.co.uk

The Hotchkin Course at Woodhall Spa was originally laid out by Harry Vardon and Harry Colt, and was later redesigned by the owner Colonel Hotchkin in the 1920s. The birch trees, heather, perfect sandy soil and cavernous bunkers mean that the course is regularly ranked as one of the best in the world. Woodhall Spa is now owned by the English Golf Union, which was established in 1924 as the governing body for men's amateur golf in England. The EGU bought Woodhall Spa in 1995, after which it created the new Bracken Course and set up the National Golf Centre.

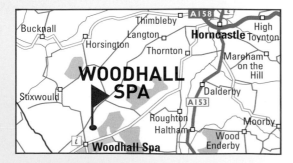

Location:
19 miles
southeast from
the centre of
Lincoln

NORTHERN
ENGLAND

THE ALWOODLEY
5m n of Leeds, West Yorkshire

1. Club founded: 1907
2. Course architect: Dr Alister MacKenzie/
   Harry S Colt
3. Type of course: Moorland
4. Length (yards): 6686
   Length (metres): 6114
5. Par: 72
6. SSS: 73
7. Membership: 450

England Photographic Atlas : Page 663, E6

Tel: (01132) 681680
www.alwoodley.co.uk

The Alwoodley was the first course to be designed by Dr Alister MacKenzie whose other achievements include Augusta National, Cypress Point and Crystal Downs in the US, and the Royal Melbourne in Australia. MacKenzie, nicknamed "the course doctor", was a founder member of The Alwoodley, which came into being when fourteen

local businessmen (including local brewer GH Tetley) realized their dream of building a new course at Wigton Moor on land leased from Lord Harewood, who became the first President of the club. MacKenzie, a GP, is quoted as saying "How frequently have I, with great difficulty, persuaded patients who were never off my doorstep to take up golf, and how rarely, if ever, have I seen them in my consulting rooms again!"

Location:
5 miles north
from
the centre of
Leeds

DE VERE SLALEY HALL
Northumberland

1. Club founded: 1988
2. Membership: 350

HUNTING COURSE
1. Course architect: David Thomas
2. Type of course: Parkland
3. Length (yards): 7073
   Length (metres): 6468
4. Par: 72
5. SSS: 71–74

PRIESTMAN COURSE
1. Course architect: Neil Coles
2. Type of course: Parkland
3. Length (yards): 7010
   Length (metres): 6410
4. Par: 72
5. SSS: 71–74

England Photographic Atlas : Page 734, D6

Tel: (01434) 673350
www.devereonline.co.uk

Slaley Hall has been described as "the Woburn of the north or the Gleneagles of the south". Certainly the latter comparison flatters the de Vere resort but, nonetheless, Slaley Hall provides two of the best courses in the north east, complemented by an excellent hotel and clubhouse. Slaley Hall, with the existing Hunting Course, was acquired in 1997 by the de Vere Group, who added a second 18-hole course, the Priestman, in 1999.

Location:
7 miles south
from the centre
of Corbridge

FAIRHAVEN
Lytham St Anne's, Lancashire

1. Club founded: 1895 (Course laid out 1922–24)
2. Course architect: Jim Steer/James Braid
3. Type of course: Links & parkland
4. Length (yards): 6883
   Length (metres): 6294
5. Par: 74
6. SSS: 73
7. Membership: 900

England Photographic Atlas : Page 629, E5

Tel: (01253) 736741

The original site of the Fairhaven Golf Club is now occupied by the Fairhaven Boating Lake – the club was ousted from the site by the expansion of the resort of St Anne's, and moved to its present home in 1924, where it provides "an interesting mix of links and parkland golf". Fairhaven hosts the Open Championship Qualifying Competitions whenever the Open itself is at Royal Lytham & St Anne's (p76), most recently in 2001.

FAIRHAVEN

Location:
1 mile east from
the centre of
Lytham St
Anne's

FILEY
North Yorkshire

1. Club founded: 1897
2. Course architect: James Braid
3. Type of course: Parkland
4. Length (yards): 6112
   Length (metres): 5589
5. Par: 70
6. SSS: 69
7. Membership: 768

England Photographic Atlas : Page 683, E5

Tel: (01723) 513293
www.mywebpage.net/fileygolf

Founded in 1897, Filey is one of Yorkshire's oldest and most respected golf clubs. The club enjoys a spectacular cliff-top setting overlooking the North Sea, with panoramic views across the expanse of Filey Bay southwards to the white cliffs of Flamborough Head and northwards to the rocky spur of Filey Brigg. It is defined as a parkland course, but Filey has the feel of a links course because of the ever-present wind, the sandy soil and the sea views. Although guides warn golfers not to expect the course of the century, Filey prides itself on its warm and friendly atmosphere and the club is described as one where members "cultivate a certain style of life".

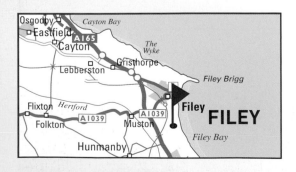

Location:
1 mile south
from
the centre of
Filey

FORMBY

Formby, Merseyside

1. Club founded: 1884 (Course completed 1895)
2. Course architect: Willie Park/Harry S Colt/
   F Pennink/Donald Steel
3. Type of course: Links
4. Length (yards): 6993
   Length (metres): 6394
5. Par: 72
6. SSS: 74
7. Membership: 600

England Photographic Atlas : Page 548, B1

Tel: (01704) 872164
www.formbygolfclub.co.uk

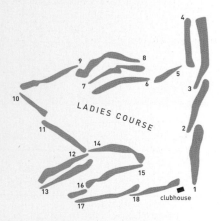

In the programme for the 1967 Amateur Championship, Ben Wright describes Formby as "'unique amongst all our great seaside courses in that it is blessed with such a profusion of pine trees, whose smell is so delicious, and whose presence does so much to soften and beautify the landscape." The trees also mean that the wind plays less of a part than at many links courses. The original course, laid out by Willie Park, followed the pattern of golf course design created at St Andrews and Westward Ho! Park's course was remodelled by Harry Colt and later lengthened by Donald Steel. Towards the end of the century, the club acquired Sutton's Farm and laid out a course for the Formby Ladies' club, which now also has its own separate clubhouse.

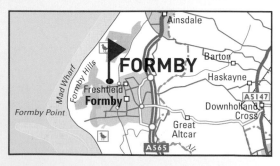

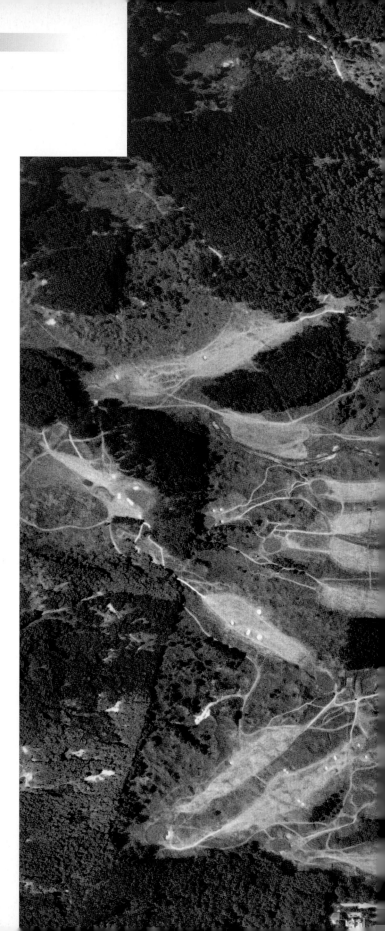

Location:
0.5 miles
northwest from
the centre of
Formby

GAINSBOROUGH
Gainsborough, Lincolnshire

1. Club founded: 1894
2. Membership: 600

THONOCK PARK COURSE
1. Course remodelled: 1986–88
2. Course architect: Remodelled by Brian Waites
3. Type of course: Parkland
4. Length (yards): 6266
   Length (metres): 5729
5. Par: 70
6. SSS: 70

KARSTEN LAKES COURSE
1. Course laid out: 1997
2. Course architect: Neil Coles
3. Type of course: Parkland
4. Length (yards): 6900
   Length (metres): 6309
5. Par: 72
6. SSS: 73

England Photographic Atlas : Page 612, A4

Tel: (01427) 613088
e-mail: emma@gainsboroughgc.co.uk

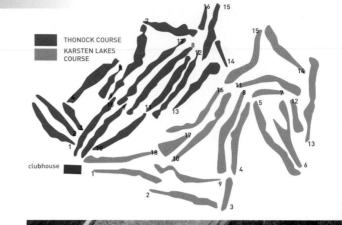

Thonock Golf Club was bought in 1985 by golf equipment manufacturer Ping and renamed Gainsborough Golf Club in March 1987. The original course (now known as Thonock Park) was remodelled by Brian Waites, and officially re-opened in September 1988 with Pro-Am and Pro-Scratch tournaments and a fly-past by the Red Arrows. In 1997, the Thonock Park course was complemented by the opening of Neil Coles's USGA specification Karsten Lakes course. Ping is the trade name of Karsten (UK) Ltd, run by Karsten Solheim, from whom the new course takes its name.

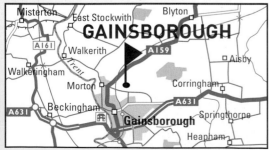

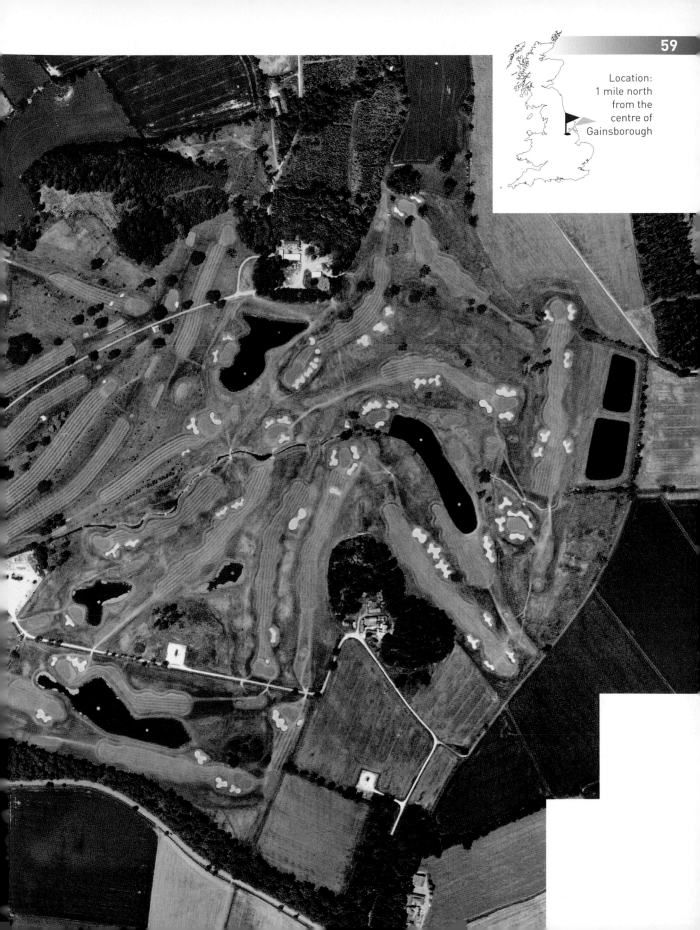

Location:
1 mile north
from the
centre of
Gainsborough

GANTON

North Yorkshire

1. Club founded: 1891
2. Course architect: Tom Chisolm, with subsequent alterations by Tom Dunn (1893)/Vardon, Ray, Braid & Taylor (1905)/Colt (various)/MacKenzie (1920s)/Cotton (1948 & 1952)/Pennick (1963)
3. Type of course: Open heathland
4. Length (yards): 6734
   Length (metres): 6158
5. Par: 73
6. SSS: 74
7. Membership: 550

England Photographic Atlas : Page 681, H5

Tel: (01944) 710329
www.gantongolfclub.com

Gary Player once said of Ganton that it is an inland course worthy of holding the Open Championship. In its early days Ganton was brought to prominence by club professional Harry Vardon's matches against JH Taylor (1896) and Willie Park Jnr (1899), and more recently it has received attention as the venue for the 2000 Curtis Cup. The club is due to host the Walker Cup in 2003, when it will become one of only three clubs to have hosted both the Ryder Cup (1949) and the Walker Cup.

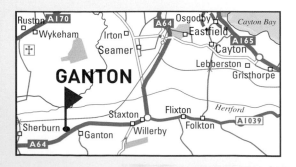

Location:
11 miles
southwest
from the centre
of Scarborough

HARROGATE
North Yorkshire

1. Club founded: 1892
2. Course architect: Sandy Herd (subsequent alterations by Dr Alister MacKenzie, 1908-11)
3. Type of course: Parkland
4. Length (yards): 6241
   Length (metres): 5707
5. Par: 69
6. SSS: 70
7. Membership: 700

England Photographic Atlas : Page 663, E3

Tel: (01423) 862999
www.harrogate-gc.co.uk

Harrogate Golf Club was founded in 1892 with a 9-hole course that opened in June of that year on part of the site now occupied by the club's near-neighbour, Oakdale Golf Club. Six years later, the club moved to its present home, once part of the ancient Forest of Knaresborough, and the new course was opened for play on May 7th 1898. Golf journalist Charles Scatchard described Harrogate as "not only one of Yorkshire's oldest courses but also one of its most attractive."

Location:
2 miles east
from the
centre of
Harrogate

HILLSIDE
Southport, Merseyside

1. Club founded: 1909 (Course laid out 1923)
2. Course architect: Remodelled by Fred Hawtree (1962)
3. Type of course: Links
4. Length (yards): 6850
   Length (metres): 6264
5. Par: 72
6. SSS: 74
7. Membership: 800

England Photographic Atlas : Page 616, D4

Tel: (01704) 567169
www.ukgolfer.org/clubs/hillside_m.html

Hillside is a course of two halves, having been extended by Fred Hawtree into duneland acquired by the club in 1962 – the first nine holes follow the line of the railway with the back nine running through the dunes. Hillside claims to be "one of the best links courses never to have hosted the Open" (a claim similar to Henry Longhurst's comment about Saunton [p. 22]), and it has certainly won high praise: Greg Norman described the back nine holes as the best in Britain, and Peter Alliss called it "one of the most scenic and testing links courses in the British Isles".

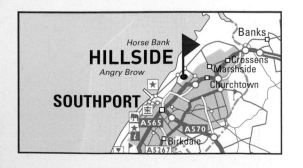

Location:
1 mile north
from the centre
of Southport

ILKLEY
West Yorkshire

1. Club founded: 1890 (Course laid out 1898)
2. Course architect: Harry S Colt/Dr Alister MacKenzie
3. Type of course: Parkland
4. Length (yards): 6260
   Length (metres): 5724
5. Par: 69
6. SSS: 70
7. Membership: 530

The River Wharfe is, without doubt, the dominating feature of this course, both in terms of the beauty of the Wharfe Valley and the famous Ilkley Moor beyond, and as a constant danger for the first seven holes of the course. Ilkley GC was founded in 1890 with a 9-hole course on Rombold's Moor, and moved to its present home by the river in 1898. Colin Montgomerie learned to play golf here, and is now an honorary life member, as is Ryder Cup Captain Mark James.

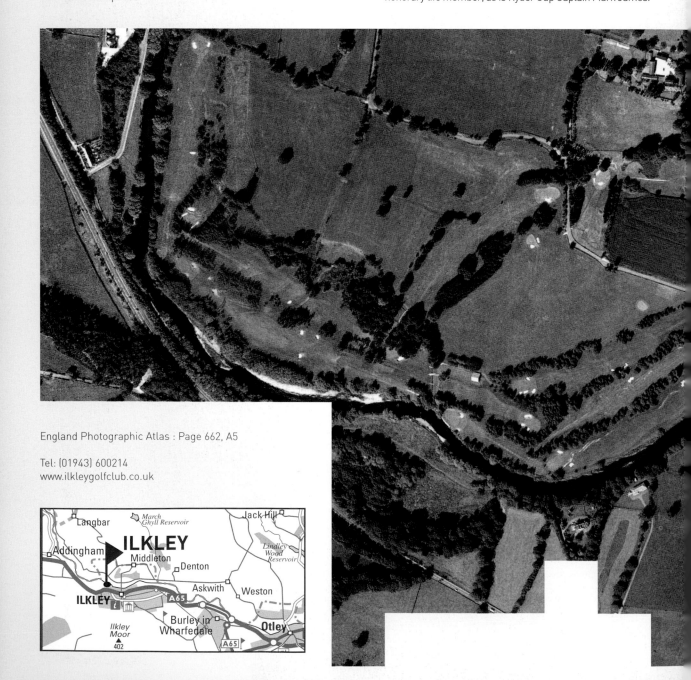

England Photographic Atlas : Page 662, A5

Tel: (01943) 600214
www.ilkleygolfclub.co.uk

Location:
1 mile west
from the
centre of Ilkley

MANCHESTER
Greater Manchester

1. Club founded: 1882 (Course laid out 1911)
2. Course architect: Harry S Colt
3. Type of course: Parkland/moorland
4. Length (yards): 6450
   Length (metres): 5898
5. Par: 72
6. SSS: 72
7. Membership: 700

England Photographic Atlas : Page 590, C1

Tel: (0161) 643 3202
www.mangc.co.uk

Manchester Golf Club was founded in 1882 as the Manchester St Andrews Golf Club, the name being chosen partly out of respect for its co-founder and first captain John Macalister, who was a member of the St Andrews Golf Club, and partly to distinguish it from the pre-existing Manchester Golf Club, which had been founded more than sixty years earlier in 1818. The year after the new club was founded, the words "St Andrews" were dropped from its name and the original Manchester Golf Club became known as "Old Manchester Golf Club", a title it retains to this day in its capacity as a club without a course. The new Manchester Golf Club's first course was a 9-hole course in the Whalley Range district but the club was soon forced to move and in 1888 relocated to Trafford Park, close to the Manchester Ship Canal. A quarter of a century later, the club was on the move again, with the course at its present home of Hopwood Park completed in 1911 and opened to members on 30th March 1912. The club bought the freehold to Hopwood Park in 1925, thus ensuring that there would be no further relocations, and extended Hopwood Cottage (the clubhouse) from 1986–87.

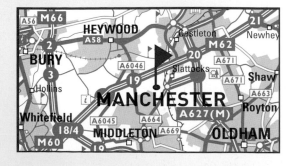

Location:
7 miles north
from the
centre of
Manchester

MOORTOWN

West Yorkshire

1. Club founded: 1909
2. Course architect: Dr Alister MacKenzie
3. Type of course: Woodland, moorland
4. Length (yards): 6826
   Length (metres): 6242
5. Par: 72
6. SSS: 74
7. Membership: 580

England Photographic Atlas : Page 640, C1

Tel: (01132) 686521
www.moortown-gc.co.uk

The founders of Moortown Golf Club invited Dr Alister MacKenzie to visit the proposed course in October 1908 and officially formed the club the following year, after MacKenzie had given the site his seal of approval. In its early days the club hosted the Yorkshire Evening News Professional Tournament and it found international prominence after the staging of the Ryder Cup here in 1929, the first English venue for the competition. There is a story that during an English Amateur Championship at Moortown, one of the players mistook the 19th hole for the 18th, and had to hit his third shot at the 18th from inside the bar!

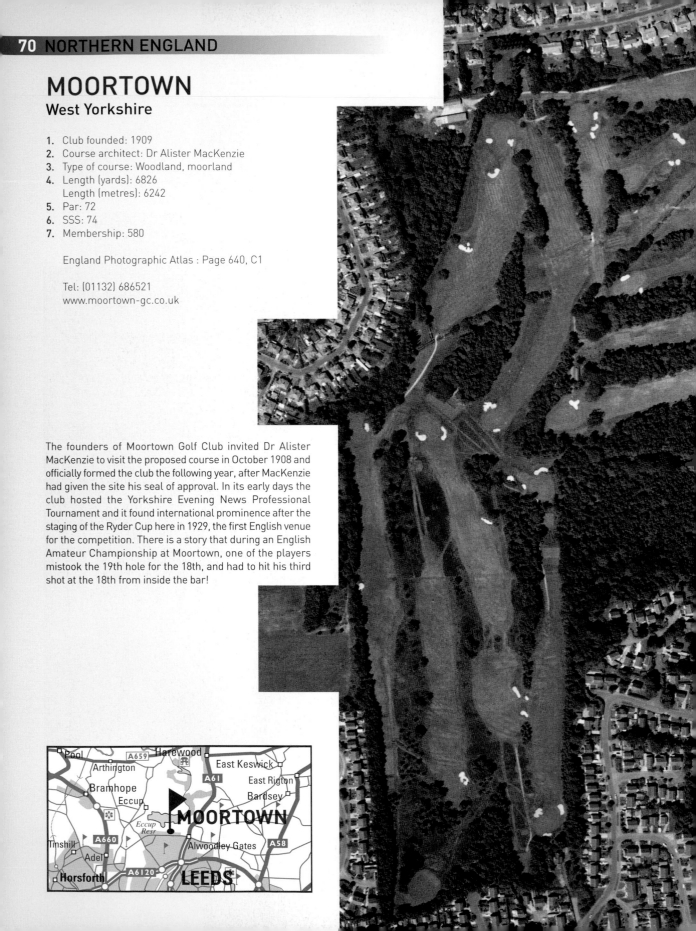

Location:
5 miles north
from the
centre of
Leeds

THE ROYAL BIRKDALE
Southport, Merseyside

1. Club founded: 1889 (Course laid out 1897)
2. Course architect: George Lowe (Remodelled by FW Hawtree and JH Taylor, 1930s)
3. Type of course: Links
4. Length (yards): 6703
   Length (metres): 6129
5. Par: 70
6. SSS: 73

England Photographic Atlas : Page 616, D4

Tel: (01704) 567920
www.royalbirkdale.com

The Royal Birkdale was founded in 1889 as the Birkdale Golf Club, and the original 9-hole course was at Shaw Hills. In 1897, the club moved the short distance to its present home at Birkdale Hills, where an 18-hole course was constructed as well as a clubhouse that subsequently had to be demolished because it had been built beyond the boundary of the ground leased by the club! During the 1930s, the course was upgraded to Championship standard, with a new clubhouse and the course itself remodelled by Hawtree and Taylor, whose philosophy was to lay out holes in the valleys between the sandhills rather than over them, giving Birkdale a reputation as one of the fairest of the championship courses. On 11th November 1951, an important notice was posted by the then captain H. F. Simpson, "I have the honour to announce that His Majesty The King, has been graciously pleased to Command that the Club shall henceforth be known as The Royal Birkdale Golf Club."

Location:
1.5 miles south
from the centre
of Southport

ROYAL LIVERPOOL (HOYLAKE)
Hoylake, Merseyside

1. Club founded: 1869
2. Course architect: Jack Morris
3. Type of course: Links
4. Length (yards): 7128
   Length (metres): 6518
5. Par: 72
6. SSS: 76
7. Membership: 810

England Photographic Atlas : Page 548, A5

Tel: (0151) 632 6757
www.royal-liverpool-golf.com

Built in 1869 on what was then the racecourse of the Liverpool Hunt Club, Hoylake is the oldest of all the English seaside courses except Westward Ho! (p. 16), which pre-dates it by five years. And like Westward Ho!, Hoylake has a reputation for belying its flat, benign appearance and being particularly difficult to play – it has even been described as "a match for Carnoustie in terms of difficulty". For the first seven years of the club's existence, the land doubled as a golf course and a race track, remembered in the names of the 1st and 18th holes, Course and Stand. The club received its Royal designation in 1871 due to the patronage of HRH The Duke of Connaught, since when Hoylake has witnessed many golfing firsts: the first Amateur Championship (1885), the first England-Scotland international (1902, later the Home Internationals) and the first GB-USA international (1921, now The Walker Cup).

ROYAL LYTHAM & ST ANNE'S
St Anne's, Lancashire

1. Club founded: 1886 (Course laid out 1897)
2. Course architect: Herbert Fowler/Harry S Colt/ T Simpson ("fine-tuned" by CK Cotton)
3. Type of course: Links
4. Length (yards): 6685
   Length (metres): 6112
5. Par: 71
6. SSS: 74
7. Membership: 600

England Photographic
Atlas : Page 628, D5

Tel: (01253) 724206
www.royallythamgolf.co.uk

Royal Lytham & St Anne's has a fearsome reputation and is often described in terms of the creatures of literature and legend: "when the wind blows, it is a monster"; "the short 5th... is a wolf in sheep's clothing"; and, most famously, American writer Art Spander described the imposing clubhouse as being "undoubtedly the former residence of Count Dracula... but you don't get really frightened until you see the golf course". And when you do get on to the course, it seems to have supernatural powers: the greens are said to reach out and push balls towards the bunkers, while Nick Edmund describes "a sea of seemingly magnetic bunkers... the Killing Fields of Royal

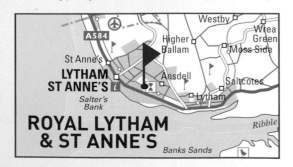

Lytham". But despite all these monstrous comparisons, Royal Lytham & St Anne's remains popular as a true challenge of golfing skills, backed up with a wealth of history and character. The club crest carries emblems of the sea but this links course lies a mile inland, the most famous reminder that it is actually near the coast being a view of Blackpool Tower from the tee of the 4th. The course has a multiple personality, partly due to the varying topography and partly because of the number of high profile course architects who have left their mark. In 2001, a number of poplar trees were removed and the complement of bunkers increased to 196, adding weight to already sound advice regarding a visit to Royal Lytham & St Anne's – bring as many sandwedges as possible.

Location:
1 mile southeast
from the centre
of Lytham St
Anne's

SEASCALE
Cumbria

1. Club founded: 1893
2. Course architect: Willie Campbell/George Lowe
3. Type of course: Links
4. Length (yards): 6416
   Length (metres): 5867
5. Par: 71
6. SSS: 71
7. Membership: 650

England Photographic Atlas : Page 684, B6

Tel: (01946) 728202
www.seascalegolfclub.org

It has been said that golf is not a matter of aesthetics, but a question of challenge – and while many would disagree, the nuclear power station and the railway line that separates this links course from the sea cannot detract from Seascale's golfing challenge.

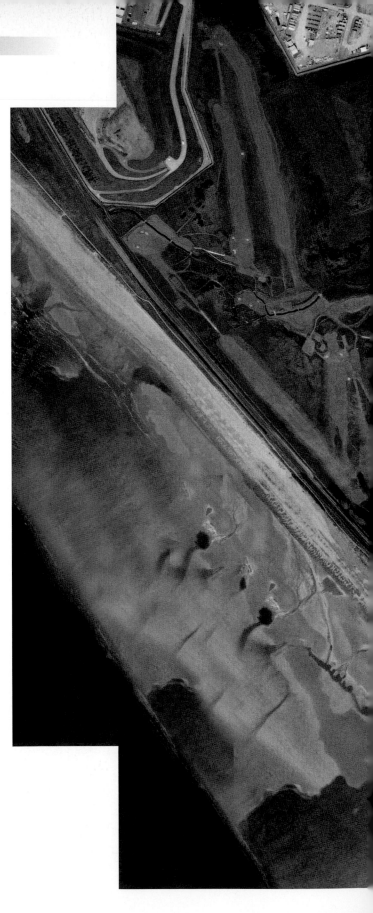

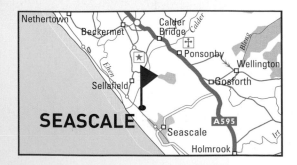

Location:
15 miles south
from the centre
of Whitehaven

SILLOTH-ON-SOLWAY
Cumbria

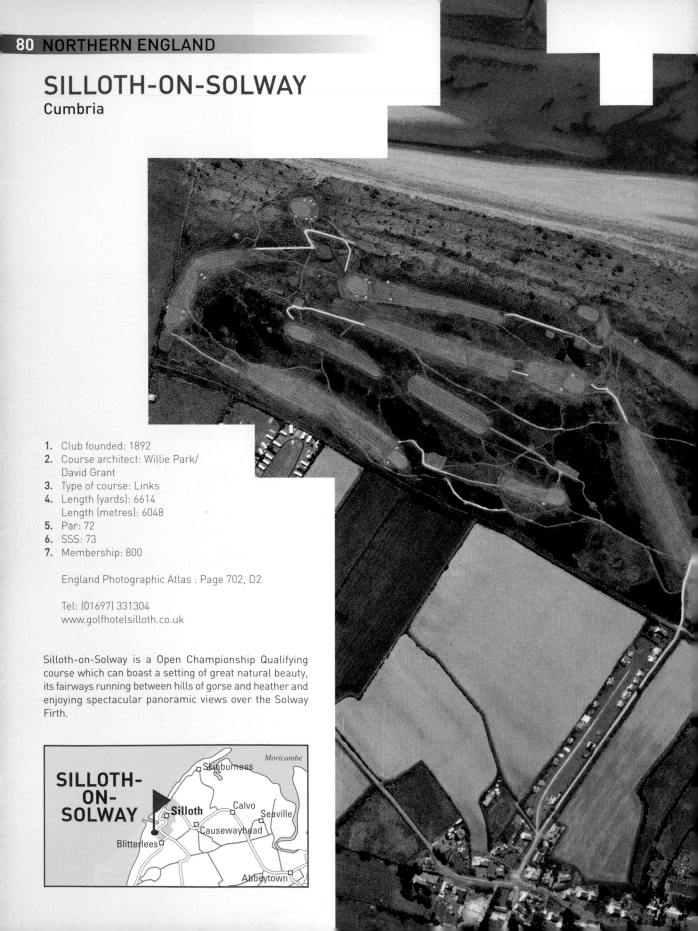

1. Club founded: 1892
2. Course architect: Willie Park/
   David Grant
3. Type of course: Links
4. Length (yards): 6614
   Length (metres): 6048
5. Par: 72
6. SSS: 73
7. Membership: 800

England Photographic Atlas : Page 702, D2

Tel: (01697) 331304
www.golfhotelsilloth.co.uk

Silloth-on-Solway is a Open Championship Qualifying
course which can boast a setting of great natural beauty,
its fairways running between hills of gorse and heather and
enjoying spectacular panoramic views over the Solway
Firth.

SILLOTH-
ON-
SOLWAY

Moricambe

Skinburness

Silloth

Calvo

Seaville

Causewayhead

Blitterlees

Abbeytown

Location:
22 miles west
from the centre
of Carlisle

ST ANNE'S OLD LINKS

Lancashire

1. Club founded: 1901
2. Course architect: Herd
3. Type of course: Links
4. Length (yards): 6616
   Length (metres): 6050
5. Par: 72
6. SSS: 72
7. Membership: 945

England Photographic Atlas : Page 638, C5

Tel: (01253) 723597
www.coastalgolf.co.uk

The St Anne's Golf Club played on a nine-hole course on this site towards the end of the 19th century but abandoned the Old Links and moved to what is now the championship course of The Royal Lytham & St Anne's Golf Club. The St Anne's Old Links GC was founded in 1901, having built a new clubhouse and extended the course to to eighteen holes over 6,046 yards. It is said that Bobby Jones, playing here in the qualifying rounds of the 1926 Open, was so impressed with the 9th that he took detailed measurements so that he could reproduce a similar hole at home in America.

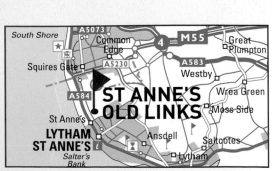

Location:
1 mile north
from the centre
of Lytham St
Anne's

SCOTLAND

BLAIRGOWRIE
Perthshire

1. Club founded: 1889
2. Membership: 1200

ROSEMOUNT COURSE
1. Course laid out: 1889
2. Course architect: Alister MacKenzie/James Braid
3. Type of course: Heathland
4. Length (yards): 6588
   Length (metres): 6024
5. Par: 72
6. SSS: 72

LANDSDOWNE COURSE
1. Course laid out: 1974
2. Course architect: Dave Thomas/Peter Alliss
3. Type of course: Heathland
4. Length (yards): 6895
   Length (metres): 6304
5. Par: 72
6. SSS: 72

Tel: (01250) 872622
www.blairgowrie-golf.co.uk

Blairgowrie was founded in 1889, with the first 9-hole course laid out on land belonging to the Dowager Marchioness of Lansdowne, from whom the course took its name, although it later became known as "The Wee Course". Old Tom Morris played the first match on the 9 hole course and afterwards said "I think this is the most beautiful inland green I have ever seen" – high praise indeed from someone of his well-travelled experience. The first 18-hole course was the famous Rosemount, designed by Alister MacKenzie, remodelled by James Braid, and complemented in 1974 by the addition of the Lansdowne, once again commemorating the Marchioness on whose land the club was founded.

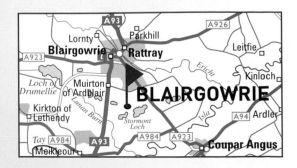

Location:
1 mile south
from the centre
of Blairgowrie

CARNOUSTIE

Angus

1. Club founded: 1842

CHAMPIONSHIP COURSE
1. Course laid out: 1857
2. Course architect: Tom Morris (Remodelled by James Braid, 1926)
3. Type of course: Links
4. Length (yards): 6941
   Length (metres): 6347
5. Par: 72
6. SSS: 75

BURNSIDE COURSE
1. Course laid out: 1914
2. Type of course: Links
3. Length (yards): 6020
   Length (metres): 5504
4. Par: 68
5. SSS: 69

BUDDON LINKS COURSE
1. Course laid out: 1981
2. Type of course: Links
3. Length (yards): 5420
   Length (metres): 4956
4. Par: 67
5. SSS: 66

Tel: (01241) 853789
www.carnoustie.co.uk

The Championship Course at Carnoustie has hosted the Open six times since the first record of golf being played here in 1650, most recently in 1999. The first club wasn't formed until nearly 200 years later, in 1842, with a ten-hole course laid out by Allan Robertson. This was later extended to 18 holes by Old Tom Morris and improved in 1926 by James Braid, since when it has remained almost unchanged. The Barry Burn, winding across the fairways, presents the greatest hazard and gives the famous 17th its name of Island. Two other courses were laid out at Carnoustie during the 20th century, the Burnside (1914) and the Buddon Links (1981).

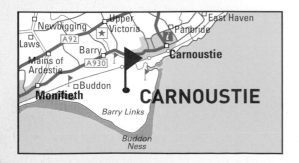

Location:
12 miles east
from the centre
of Dundee

CRUDEN BAY
Aberdeenshire

1. Club founded: 1899
2. Course architect: Old Tom Morris & Archie Simpson
   (Redesigned by Tom Simpson & Herbert Fowler, 1926)
3. Type of course: Links
4. Length (yards): 6395
   Length (metres): 5847
5. Par: 70
6. SSS: 72
7. Membership: 1070

Tel: (01779) 812285
www.crudenbaygolfclub.co.uk

There is evidence that there was a golf club in Cruden Bay
as early as 1791, but the present club was not founded until
over a century later. This club's original course was
commissioned by the Great North of Scotland Railway
(GNSR), which also built the Cruden Bay Hotel (since
demolished) in order to stimulate tourism at a time when
the railway company was promoting the Moray Firth as the
Scottish Riviera. The hotel and golf course were served by
an electric tramway from the local station and became
known as "the Brighton of the North". The GNSR's course
was designed by Old Tom Morris and opened in 1899: the
present course stands on the same site and incorporates
many of Morris's original features.

Location:
22 miles
northeast from
the centre of
Aberdeen

THE GLENEAGLES HOTEL
Perthshire

PGA CENTENARY COURSE (PREVIOUSLY MONARCH)
1. Course laid out: 1993
2. Course architect: Jack Nicklaus
3. Type of course: Moorland
4. Length (yards): 7081
   Length (metres): 6475
5. Par: 72
6. SSS: 74

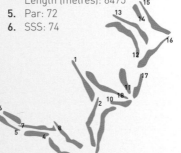

KING'S COURSE
1. Course laid out 1919
2. Course architect: James Braid (assisted by CK Hutchinson)
3. Type of course: Moorland
4. Length (yards): 6790
   Length (metres): 6209
5. Par: 70
6. SSS: 71

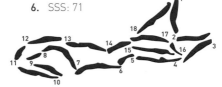

QUEEN'S COURSE
1. Course laid out 1919
2. Course architect: James Braid
3. (assisted by CK Hutchinson)
4. Type of course: Moorland
   Length (yards): 5965
5. Length (metres): 5455
6. Par: 68
7. SSS: 69

1. Club founded: 1919

Tel: (01764) 694469
www.gleneagles.com

Another golf resort that owes its existence to a railway company is Gleneagles, the brainchild of Donald Matheson, who was General Manager of the Caledonian Railway Company. The first two golf courses opened in 1919 and the hotel in 1924. Of the three championship courses at Gleneagles, King's is universally considered the finest, described by the hotel as having "tested the aristocracy of golf, both professional and amateur" and by architect James Braid as the pinnacle of his career. The other two courses perfectly complement the colossus that is King's: the natural beauty of the Queen's is an inspiration to golfers from around the world, and would almost certainly have received far greater recognition if it stood alone rather than being seen as "the second course at Gleneagles". The Monarch, designed by Jack Nicklaus in 1993 and renamed the PGA Centenary in 2001, provides a great contrast and caters for an American style of play.

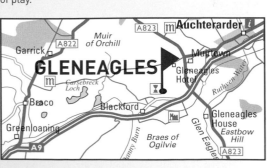

Location:
16 miles
southwest from
the centre of
Perth

KINGSBARNS
Fife

1. Club founded: 2001
2. Course architect: Kyle Phillips/Mark Parsinen
3. Type of course: Links
4. Length (yards): 7126
   Length (metres): 6516
5. Par: 72

Tel: (01334) 460860
www.kingsbarns.com

Golf at Kingsbarns dates back to 1793, although this highly-rated links course wasn't created until the dawn of the 21st century. The terrain is perfect for golf, with sandy soil, undulating ridges and hollows, and the Cambo Burn running into the North Sea, which can be seen from almost every hole on the course.

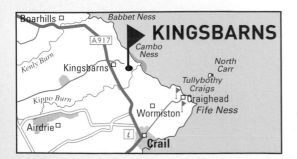

Location:
0.5 miles east
from the centre
of Kingsbarns

LOCH LOMOND
Dunbartonshire

1. Club founded: 1993
2. Course architect: Tom Weiskopf/Jay Morrish
3. Type of course: Parkland
4. Length (yards): 7060
   Length (metres): 6456
5. Par: 71

Tel: (01436) 655555
www.lochlomond.com

The short history of the exclusive Loch Lomond Golf Club is intimately entwined with the centuries-old history of the Clan Colquhoun, on whose 50,000 acre estate the 660 acre course is laid out. Rossdhu manor house, built by the Colquhouns in 1773 to replace Rossdhu Castle, is now the clubhouse, while the ruins of the 15th century castle form the backdrop to Loch Lomond's 18th green. The club owners, US-based companies Lyle Anderson and DMB, claim to "deeply appreciate the opportunity they have been given to create an international private club on such hallowed ground", but the club's exclusivity has ruffled a few feathers in a country where golf has always been seen as the right of the masses rather than the privilege of the few – and one criticism of the otherwise acclaimed course is that it is "a little too American for this part of the world".

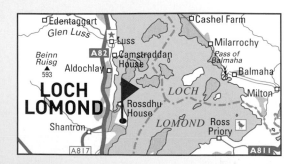

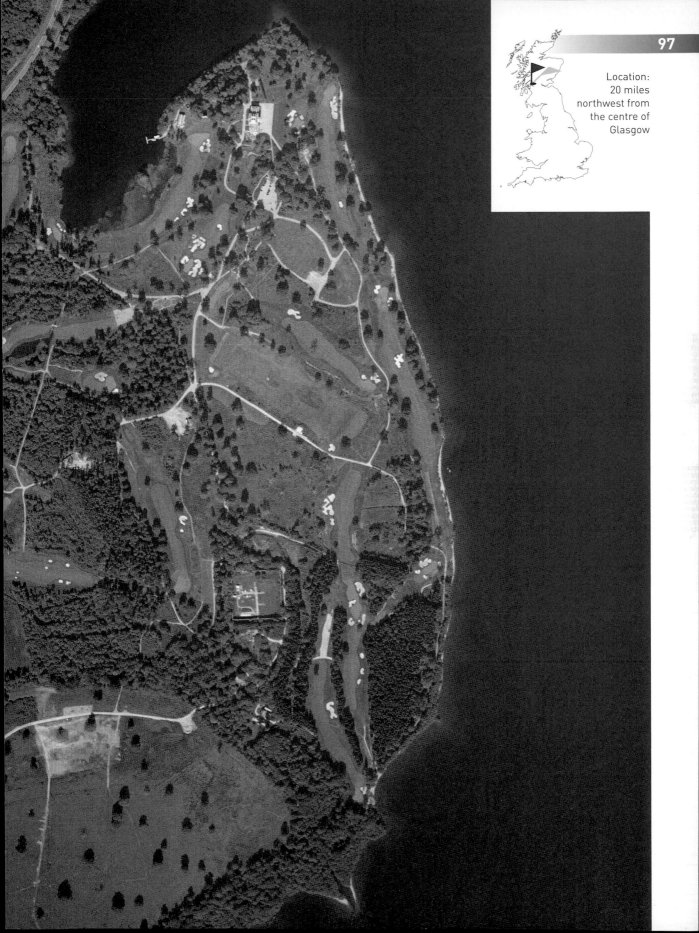

Location:
20 miles
northwest from
the centre of
Glasgow

MUIRFIELD (THE HONOURABLE COMPANY OF EDINBURGH GOLFERS)

Edinburgh

1. Club founded: 1744
2. Course laid out: 1891
3. Course architect: Tom Morris (Remodelled by Harry S Colt & Tom Simpson, 1920s)
4. Type of course: Links
5. Length (yards): 6601
   Length (metres): 6036
6. Par: 73
7. SSS: 73
   Membership: 625

   Tel: (01620) 842123

It is an accepted fact that the Royal & Ancient administers golf from St Andrews but things could have been very different – the first set of rules was compiled in 1744 by the Honourable Company of Edinburgh Golfers, the world's oldest golf club, and Muirfield could easily have become the spiritual home of the game (or Leith Links, or Musselburgh, which were the previous homes of the HCEG). A copy of the original "thirteen rules of golf" is displayed in the clubhouse at Muirfield. The course, whose layout of two concentric rings of nine holes each is clearly visible in this photograph has hosted 11 Open championships, the first in 1892 within a year of the course opening, and the most recent 110 years later in 2002.

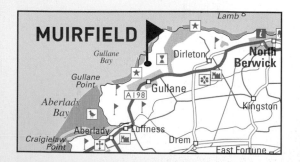

MUIRFIELD

Lamb
Gullane Bay
Dirleton
North Berwick
Gullane Point
Gullane
A198
Kingston
Aberlady Bay
Luffness
Aberlady
Drem
Craigielaw Point
East Fortune

Location:
18 miles east
from the centre
of Edinburgh

NAIRN
Highland

1. Club founded: 1887
2. Course architect: Old Tom Morris/James Braid/ Archie Simpson
3. Type of course: Links
4. Length (yards): 6732
   Length (metres): 6156
5. Par: 72
6. SSS: 74
7. Membership: 1100

Tel: (01667) 453208
www.nairngolfclub.co.uk

Nairn Golf Club describes its renowned course in a very understated manner simply as a "traditional Scottish golf links course". The heather, broom and gorse make for a challenging course with extensive views over the Moray Firth. The original course, laid out in 1887 when the club was founded, has since been extended by Archie Simpson, Old Tom Morris and James Braid, and it is now considered to be one of the best courses in the United Kingdom.

Location:
15 miles east
from the centre
of Inverness

NORTH BERWICK
Lothian

1. Club founded: 1832
2. Course architect: Unknown
3. Type of course: Links
4. Length (yards): 6420
   Length (metres): 5870
5. Par: 71
6. SSS: 71
7. Membership: 324

Tel: (01620) 892135

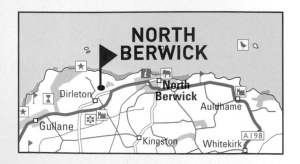

North Berwick is among the oldest golf clubs in the world, and numbers among its founder members a soldier who fought at Waterloo. The course is described by the Peugeot Golf Guide as being "at once archaic and very modern", and it retains something of the atmosphere of golf in the early days of the club – the opening holes run along a raised beach varying between 10 and 30 feet above sea level, where golfers must "avoid passers-by who watch without a smile". The club originally played on a 6-hole course, extended first to 7 holes and then to 18 in 1877. Probably the most famous hole on the course is "Redan", the "diabolical and often imitated" 15th, which is said to be most frequently copied short hole in the world. Past captains of this prestigious club include former British Prime Minister Arthur J Balfour, who was known as the "Father of English Golf" – indeed, his love of golf was so well-known that Punch magazine called him "Arthur Golfour".

Location:
0.5 miles west
from the centre
of North
Berwick

PRESTWICK
Ayrshire

1. Club founded: 1851
2. Course architect: Unknown
3. Type of course: Links
4. Length (yards): 6668
   Length (metres): 6098
5. Par: 72
6. SSS: 73
7. Membership: 580

Tel: (01292) 477404
www.prestwickgc.co.uk

Like many sports clubs and governing bodies, Prestwick Golf Club was founded in a pub – in this case Prestwick's Red Lion Inn. Old Tom Morris was the first Keeper of the Green, having been head-hunted from St Andrew's where he returned in 1864. Morris was four times winner of the Open Championship, a competition initiated by Prestwick GC and the first eleven of which were held here from 1860–72 (no competition in 1871). In 1872, together with the Royal & Ancient and the Honourable Company of Edinburgh Golfers, Prestwick bought the silver Claret Jug for which the Open is now played, but the club which initiated and nurtured the competition was removed from the rota of courses after the 1925 Open. Whether this was because of deficiences in the course or because the crowd mobbed leader MacDonald Smith, causing him to fall behind in the final round, is uncertain, but Prestwick has never hosted an Open since.

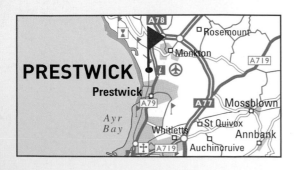

Location:
0.5 miles north
from the centre
of Prestwick

ROYAL TROON
Ayrshire

1. Club founded: 1878
2. Membership: 800

OLD COURSE
1. Course architect: George Strath/ Willie Fernie
2. Type of course: Links
3. Length (yards): 7097
   Length (metres): 6490
4. Par: 71
5. SSS: 74

PORTLAND COURSE (PREVIOUSLY THE RELIEF COURSE)
1. Course laid out 1895
2. Course architect: Willie Fernie
3. Type of course: Links
4. Length (yards): 6289
   Length (metres): 5748
5. Par: 71
6. SSS: 71

Tel: (01292) 311555
www.royaltroon.co.uk

Royal Troon's motto "Tam Arte Quam Marte", more by skill than effort, is said to encapsulate the ideals of golf, and plenty of skill is required on the difficult Old Course which includes the famous (or notorious) Postage Stamp. This course includes both the longest and the shortest holes of the entire Open rota, the 6th being 577 yds and the 8th (the Postage Stamp), being 126 yds. Despite its legendary difficulty the Postage Stamp was holed in one in the 1973 Open by Gene Sarazen, 41 years after he had first won the competition (at Sandwich) in 1932. Troon GC was awarded Royal status in 1978, its centenary year, and became the most recent club to be so honoured and the only one to have been granted the honour by Elizabeth II.

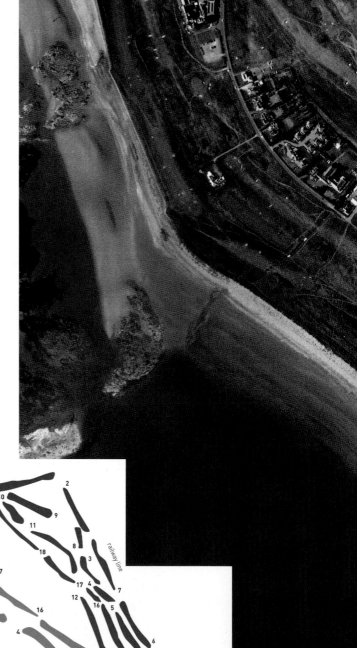

OLD COURSE

PORTLAND COURSE

Location:
1 miles south
from the centre
of Troon

ST ANDREWS
Fife

1. Club founded: 15th century
2. Membership: Public course

OLD COURSE
1. Course laid out: 15th century
2. Course architect: Unknown
3. Type of course: Links
4. Length (yards): 6566
   Length (metres): 6004
5. Par: 72
6. SSS: 72

NEW COURSE
1. Course laid out: 1895
2. Course architect: W Hall Blyth/Old Tom Morris
   Type of course: Links
3. Length (yards): 6604
4. Length (metres): 6039
   Par: 71
5. SSS: 72

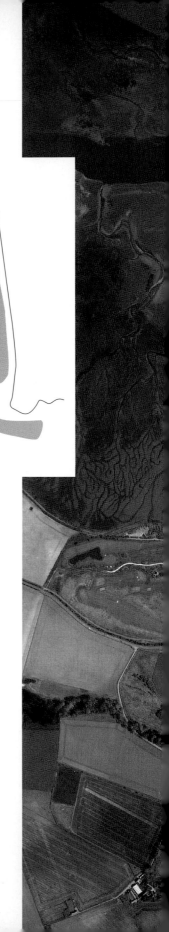

St Andrews is the spiritual home of golf, the game almost certainly having been played here since the 12th century (although there is no documentary evidence) and the present Old Course being dated to the 15th. Although St Andrews is famously the home of the Royal & Ancient Golf Club, all five courses are public and the R&A does not own its own course. The links land is publicly owned and since 1974 the courses have been operated and maintained by the St Andrews Links Trust, although members of the six St Andrews clubs have privileges and playing rights. The Old Course is known as the home of golf and has hosted the Open on 26 occasions, beating Prestwick's record of 24; only four of the holes have their own greens, the remaining seven shared greens recalling the early days of golf when the same nine holes would be played out and in. The R&A was founded as the Society of St Andrews Golfers in 1754, became the Royal & Ancient in 1834 by decree of William IV, and as well as being a private club is now also the governing body of golf worldwide (except in the US and Mexico), administering the rules and, more recently, organizing the Open.

EDEN COURSE
1. Course laid out: 1914
2. Course architect: Harry S Colt
3. Type of course: Links
4. Length (yards): 6112
   Length (metres): 5588
5. Par: 70
6. SSS: 70

JUBILEE COURSE
1. Course laid out: 1897
2. Course architect: Old Tom Morris/Auchterlonie/Steel/Angus
3. Type of course: Links
4. Length (yards): 6805
   Length (metres): 6222
5. Par: 72
6. SSS: 73

Tel: (01334) 466666
www.standrews.org.uk

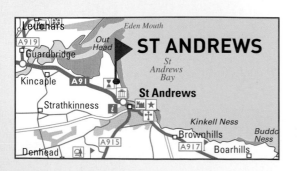

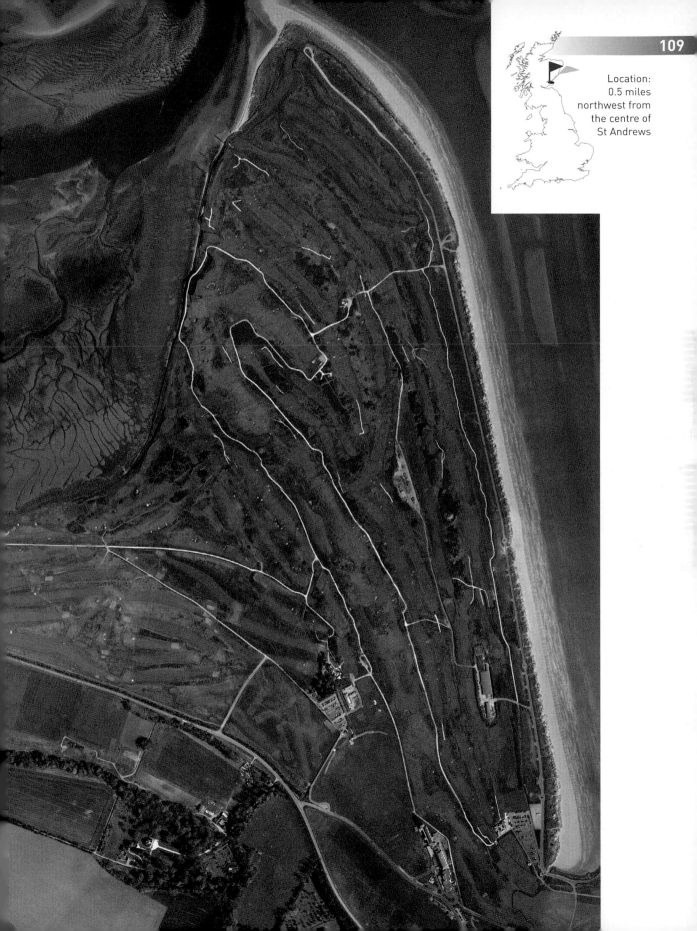

Location:
0.5 miles
northwest from
the centre of
St Andrews

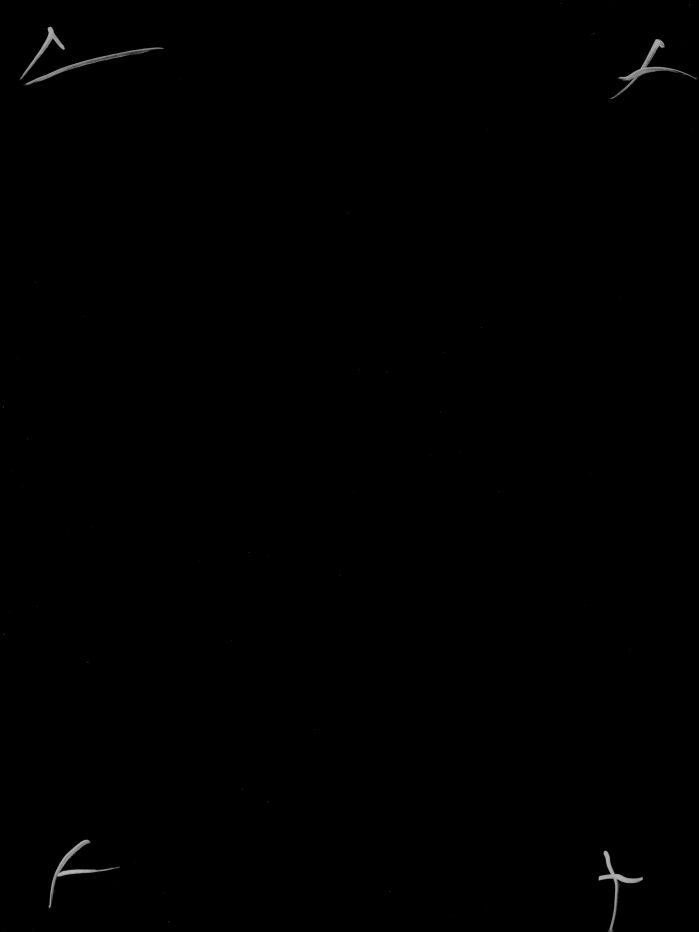

WALES AND
NORTHERN
IRELAND

BANGOR
County Down

1. Club founded: 1903
2. Course architect: James Braid
3. Type of course: Inland
4. Length (yards): 6424
   Length (metres): 5874
5. Par: 71
6. SSS: 71
7. Membership: 1100

   Tel: (028) 9127 0922

Bangor Golf Club was founded in 1903 with a 9-hole golf course which was extended to 18 holes by James Braid in 1905. The course boasts stunning views of Belfast Lough, particularly from the 4th, and the view from the clubhouse is unsurpassed. Bangor has played host to a number of events including Pro-Am tournaments and the Ulster and Irish Professional Championships.

Location:
1 miles south
from the centre
of Bangor

CELTIC MANOR HOTEL
Newport

1. Club founded:1994
2. Membership: 200

Tel: (01633) 413000
www.celtic-manor.com

COLDRA WOODS COURSE
1. Course laid out: 1994–95
2. Course architect: Robert Trent Jones Snr
3. Type of course: Parkland
4. Length (yards): 4094
   Length (metres): 3744
5. Par: 61
6. SSS: 60

ROMAN ROAD COURSE
1. Course laid out: 1992–95
2. Course architect: Robert Trent Jones Snr
3. Type of course: Parkland
4. Length (yards): 7001
   Length (metres): 6401
5. Par: 70
6. SSS: 74

WENTWOOD HILLS COURSE
1. Course laid out: 1994–99
2. Course architect: Robert Trent Jones Jnr
3. Type of course: Parkland
4. Length (yards): 7403
   Length (metres): 6770
5. Par: 72
6. SSS: 77

The Celtic Manor Hotel is the brainchild of one man who was prepared to spend £100m to realize his vision. Sir Terence Matthews, who was born in the Manor House when it was in use as a maternity hospital, bought the abandoned 19th-century mansion in the 1970s, opened a successful hotel and then set about creating the golf courses. Having met Robert Trent Jones Snr in Florida and discovered his Welsh roots, Matthews invited him to Celtic Manor where, from 1992, they planned the Roman Road course – so named because it is criss-crossed with Roman roads. The Coldra Woods course was built around the site of a hilltop Roman military camp, and Wentwood Hills alongside the River Usk. Celtic Manor is the home of the Wales Open, and is scheduled to host the Ryder Cup in 2010 on its first visit to Wales.

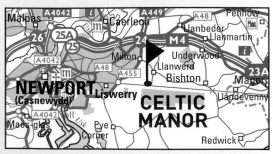

Location:
2 miles east
from the centre
of Newport

THE KNOCK
Belfast

1. Club founded: 1895
2. Course architect: Harry S Colt/MacKenzie/Allison
3. Type of course: Parkland
4. Length (yards): 6407
   Length (metres): 5859
5. Par: 70
6. SSS: 71
7. Membership: 900

   Tel: (028) 9048 3251

The Knock Club was founded in 1895 with a small 9-hole course close to the old Knock Railway Station. Within three years the club had moved to a new 9-hole course at nearby Shandon Park, whose wooded hill is still depicted on the club crest, despite the fact that in 1920 the club moved again, to an 18-hole course at the present location of Summerfield on the outskirts of Belfast. The course, which has magnificent views of Stormont Castle, incorporated the mature trees and meandering streams of the Summerfield estate which still provide a peaceful atmosphere for golfers to this day – although the calming effects of these natural features only remain calming whilst the ball remains on the fairway or the green rather than among the trees or in the water. At the 6th is a 70-foot monkey puzzle tree, said to be the oldest in the British Isles, and close to the 11th green is a chalybeate spring said to have medicinal qualities: no doubt course architect Dr MacKenzie would have approved.

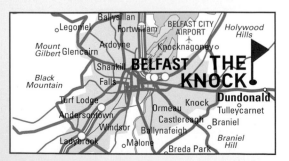

Location:
4 miles east
from the
centre of
Belfast

THE NEWPORT

Newport

1. Club founded: 1903
2. Course architect: Unknown
3. Type of course: Parkland
4. Length (yards): 6431
   Length (metres): 5881
5. Par: 72
6. SSS: 71
7. Membership: 800

Tel: (01633) 892643

www.welcome.to/newport_golf_club

The Newport was founded in 1903 at Ladyhill in Newport, but less than a decade later the site was acquired for a housing development and in 1912 the club was forced to move to its present location at Great Oak. The area is named after the mighty Golynos Oak that once stood here and was felled in 1810, yielding 2,426 cubic feet of timber and six tons of bark. The course itself is laid out some 300 feet above sea level on an inland plateau, sheltered from the weather by the trees of Llwyni Wood and with views south across the Bristol Channel towards the hills of Devon and Somerset and north-east towards the hills of North Gwent and the Brecon Beacons. The Newport is renowned for its varied layout over a gently rolling landscape, and for the quality of its green-keeping – the greens and tees are watered by a system fed from the club's own borehole.

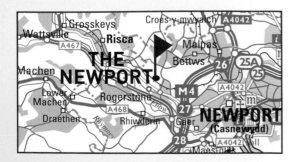

Location:
3 miles west
from the
centre of
Newport

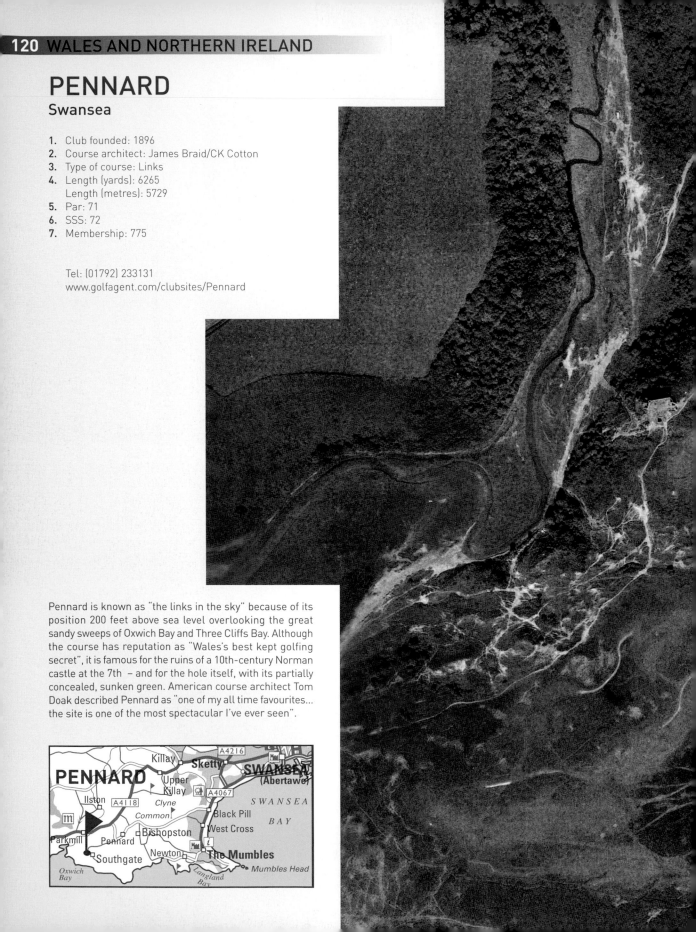

PENNARD

Swansea

1. Club founded: 1896
2. Course architect: James Braid/CK Cotton
3. Type of course: Links
4. Length (yards): 6265
   Length (metres): 5729
5. Par: 71
6. SSS: 72
7. Membership: 775

Tel: (01792) 233131
www.golfagent.com/clubsites/Pennard

Pennard is known as "the links in the sky" because of its position 200 feet above sea level overlooking the great sandy sweeps of Oxwich Bay and Three Cliffs Bay. Although the course has reputation as "Wales's best kept golfing secret", it is famous for the ruins of a 10th-century Norman castle at the 7th – and for the hole itself, with its partially concealed, sunken green. American course architect Tom Doak described Pennard as "one of my all time favourites... the site is one of the most spectacular I've ever seen".

ROYAL BELFAST
County Antrim & County Down

1. Club founded: 1881 (Course laid out 1925)
2. Course architect: Harry S Colt
3. Type of course: Parkland
4. Length (yards): 6184
   Length (metres): 5655
5. Par: 71
6. SSS: 70
7. Membership: 1200

Tel: (028) 9042 8165
www.royalbelfast.com

Founded on November 9th 1881, the Royal Belfast is the oldest club in the country and so claims its place in golfing history as the origin of the game in Ireland. The first course (laid out in just seven weeks) was at Kinnegar, before the club moved to Carnalea near Bangor in 1892 and then to its present home on 140 acres of land at Craigavad in 1925. One of only four golf clubs in Ireland with royal status, the honour was bestowed in 1885 by the Prince of Wales (later Edward VII) who became the club's first patron, a position now held by the Duke of York (Prince Andrew).

Location:
6 miles east
from the centre
of Belfast

ROYAL PORTHCAWL
Cardiff

1. Club founded: 1891 (Course laid out c. 1898)
2. Course architect: Charles Gibson
3. Type of course: Links
4. Length (yards): 6685
   Length (metres): 6113
5. Par: 72
6. SSS: 74
7. Membership: 800

Tel: (01656) 782251
www.golf-in-wales.com

Royal Porthcawl overlooks the Bristol Channel, with views south to Somerset and Exmoor, and northwest across Swansea Bay to the Gower Peninsula. The club was founded in 1891 at Lock's Common, moving to its present location in 1898. Royal status was bestowed in 1909 by Edward VII. Tom Scott, former editor of Golf Illustrated, described Royal Porthcawl as one of the twelve finest courses in the world, and Michael Williams of the Daily Telegraph wrote that the club "epitomises all that is best about the game, as it once was, even down to a creaking clubhouse that is as unchanging as the magnificent links and unrivalled hospitality."

Location:
22 miles west
from the centre
of Cardiff

ROYAL ST DAVID'S

Gwynedd

1. Club founded: 1894
2. Course architect: Unknown
3. Type of course: Links
4. Length (yards): 6571
   Length (metres): 6009
5. Par: 69
6. SSS: 73
7. Membership: 780

Tel: (01766) 780361
www.royalstdavids.co.uk

Royal St David's occupies a stunning position on the dune-land between Harlech Castle and the sea, with views of the Snowdon Mountains, the medieval castle and (from the 16th tee), the Lleyn Peninsular across Tremadog Bay. It was the heroic defence of the castle during the Wars of Roses that inspired the song "Men of Harlech". Unusually, the course, which has been described as the toughest par 69 in the world, has been designated a Site of Special Scientific Interest for the orchids that grow in the rough.

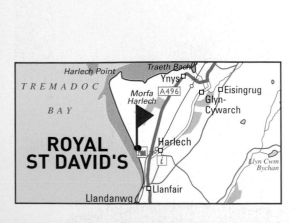

index

Allen, Sir Peter, 30
Allison, 116
Alliss, Peter, 12, 34, 36, 42, 64, 86
Alwoodley, the, 48
Ashford, 10
Baird, John, 38
Balfour, Arthur J., 102
Balfour, Earl, 38
Bangor, 112
Barnstaple, 22
Barry Burn, 88
Belfast, 116
Belfast Lough, 112
Belfry, the, 34
Bideford, 16
Birkdale Hills, 72
Blackpool Tower, 76
Blairgowrie, 86
Blyth, W. Hall, 108
Bonsor, Sir Cosmo, 26
Bournemouth, 12
Braid, James, 26, 52, 54, 60, 86, 88, 92, 100, 112, 120
Braunton Burrows, 22
Broadwater Lake, 36
Brocket Hall, 36
Burnham & Berrow, 8
Burnham-on-Sea, 8
Caledonian Railway Company, 92
Callender, Colin, 22
Campbell, Guy, 14, 30, 38
Campbell, Willie, 78
Cardiff, 124
Carnoustie, 10, 74, 88
Celtic Manor Hotel, 114
Chart Hills, 10
Chisolm, Tom, 60
Chobham Common, 24
Churchill, Winston, 26
Clan Colquhoun, 96
Clark, Clive, 36, 42
Coles, Neil, 50, 58
Colt, Harry S., 20, 24, 28, 44, 48, 56, 60, 66, 68, 76, 98, 116, 122
Connaught, Duke of, 74
Cotton, C.K., 76, 120
Cotton, Henry, 38, 60
Coventry, 40
Craigavad, 122
Cruden Bay, 90
Darwin, Bernard, 14, 18
De Vere Slaley Hall, 50
Deal (Royal Cinque Ports), 14
Doak, Tom, 120
Dobereiner, Peter, 26
Dunn, Tom, 14, 38, 60
Edmund, Nick, 10, 34, 76
Edward VII, 124
Elcho, Lord, 38
Elizabeth II, 106
Fairhaven, 52
Faldo, Nick, 10
Felixstowe Ferry, Martello Course, 38
Ferndown Old Course, 12
Fernie, Willie, 106
Fife, 94, 108
Filey, 54
Formby, 56
Fowler, Herbert, 16, 22, 26, 76, 90
Gainsborough, 58
Gallacher, Bernard, 28
Ganton, 60

George, Lloyd, 26
Gibson, Charles, 124
Gleneagles Hotel, 50, 92
Golf Monthly, 22
Grant, David, 80
Gwynedd, 126
Harewood, Lord, 48
Harlech Castle, 126
Harrogate, 62
Hawtree, F.W., 64, 72
Hay, 42
Herd, Sandy, 62, 82
Hillside, 64
Hilton, Harold, 12
Honourable Company of Edinburgh Golfers, 98, 104
Hopwood Park, 68
Hotchkin, Col S.V., 44
Hoylake (Royal Liverpool), 74
Hutchinson, Cecil K., 30, 92
Ilkley, 66
Jacobs, John, 28
James, Henry, 20
James, Mark, 66
Jones, Bobby, 24, 82
Jones, Robert Trent Snr, 114
Karsten Lakes, 58
Kingsbarns, 94
Knock, the, 116
Lamb, Henry, 18
Lansdowne, Dowager Marchioness of, 86
Lawrie, Charles, 42
Loch Lomond, 96
Longhurst, Henry, 22, 64
Lothian, 102
Lowe, George, 72, 78
Lyle Anderson, 96
Lytham St Anne's, 52
Macalister, John, 68
MacKenzie, Dr Alister, 48, 60, 62, 66, 70, 86, 116
Manchester, 68
Marriott Forest of Arden, 40
Matheson, Donald, 92
Matthews, Sir Terence, 114
McMurray, 42
Melbourne, Lord, 36
Montgomerie, Colin, 66
Moortown, 70
Moray Firth, 90, 100
Morris, Jack, 74
Morris, Tom, 16, 86, 88, 90, 98, 100, 108
Morrish, Jay, 96
Muirfield, 10, 98
Nairn, 100
Newport, 118
Nicklaus, Jack, 92
Norman, Greg, 64
North Berwick, 102
Oakdale Golf Club, 62
Packington Estate, 40
Palmerston, Lord, 36
Park Junior, Willie, 24, 56, 80
Parsinen, Mark, 94
Pegwell Bay, 18
Pennard, 120
Pennink, F., 18, 56
Pennink, J.J., 22
Peugeot Golf Guide, 20
Phillips, Kyle, 94
Pine Valley, 10
Ping, 58

Player, Gary, 24, 28
Prestwick, 18, 104, 108
Pulborough (West Sussex), 30
Purves, Dr W. Laidlaw, 18
Ray, 60
River Lea, 36
River Wharfe, 66
Robertson, Allan, 88
Rombold's Moor, 66
Rossdhu, 96
Royal & Ancient Golf Club, 108
Royal Belfast, 122
Royal Birkdale, the, 72
Royal Cinque Ports (Deal), 14
Royal Liverpool (Hoylake), 74
Royal Lytham & St Anne's, 52, 76, 82
Royal Melbourne, 10
Royal North Devon (Westward Ho!), 16
Royal Porthcawl, 124
Royal St David's, 126
Royal St George's, 18
Royal Troon, 106
Ryder Cup, 34, 66, 70, 114
Rye, 20
Sandwich, 18
Sarazen, Gene, 106
Saunton, 22
Scatchard, Charles, 62
Scott, Tom, 124
Seascale, 78
Shaw Hills, 72
Silloth-on-Solway, 80
Simpson, Archie, 90, 100
Simpson, H.F., 72
Simpson, T., 76, 90, 98
Smith, MacDonald, 104
Smyers, Steven, 10
Society of St Andrews Golfers, 108
Southport, 64
Spander, Art, 76
St Andrews, 18, 22, 56, 98, 104, 108
St Anne's Old Links, 82
Steel, Donald, 36, 40, 56
Steer, Jim, 52
Strath, George, 106
Sunningdale, 24
Sutton's Farm, 56
Swansea, 120
Tarrant, Walter George, 28
Taw, the, 22
Taylor, J.H., 26, 60, 72
Thomas, David, 34, 50, 86
Torridge estuary, 22
Trafford Park, 68
Vardon, Harry, 22, 26, 44, 60
Waites, Brian, 58
Wales, Prince of, 26, 122
Walton Heath, 26
Webb, Sir Henry, 12
Weiskopf, Tom, 96
Welwyn, 36
Wentworth, 28
West Sussex (Pulborough), 30
Westward Ho! (Royal North Devon), 16, 56, 74
Whalley Range district, 68
Wigton Moor, 48
Woburn, 42, 50
Woodhall Spa, 44
Wright, Ben, 56
York, Duke of, 26, 122